BROKEN CHILD | BROKEN GIRL | BROKEN WOMAN
Copyright © 2023 Dr. Janis Smith
All rights reserved. No portion of this book may be reproduced, stored in a retrieval system, or transmitted in any form or by any means—electronic, mechanical, photocopy, recording, scanning, or other—except for brief quotations in critical reviews or articles, without prior written permission of the author.

Published by
Angels Trail Publishing
Saint Cloud, Florida
www.angelstrail.com

ISBN: 979-8-218-14447-0   1 2 3 4 5 6 7 8 9 10

Printed in the United States of America

JANIS SMITH

BROKEN CHILD
BROKEN GIRL
BROKEN WOMAN

This book is dedicated to my husband, Dr. Gary Smith, who modeled Jesus as a loving man, husband, father and friend for over 5 decades. Thank you, darling, for believing in my story, and even pushing me to greater heights than I could ever imagine. I also want to thank my family, Dr. Jeffrey and Amy Smith, Tyler and Jen Smith, Stacey Smith, and my grandchildren Mia, Jude and Zoe. I cannot fail to mention my dear brother, Michael Flippo, who has been with me from the beginning. Special recognition to Mark Greenaway (Saint Cloud, Florida) for his exceptional illustrations.

CONTENTS

PREFACE ix

INTRODUCTION 11

CHAPTER 1. COAL MINER'S DAUGHTER 13

CHAPTER 2. ALABAMY BOUND. 25

CHAPTER 3. THE RIVER 43

CHAPTER 4. FORAYED. 59

CHAPTER 5. ANGEL'S TRAIL. 73

CHAPTER 6. SCHOOL, RULES and MORES 85

CHAPTER 7. FROZEN 101

CHAPTER 8. THE WHIPPING 117

CHAPTER 9. CHANGES 127

CHAPTER 10. AN ENGAGING SEASON 143

CHAPTER 11. THE GUN CHANGES HANDS 159

CHAPTER 12. MEMORIES 177

CHAPTER 13. WHITE ELEPHANT IN THE ROOM. 187

CHAPTER 14. FATHER, FORGIVE ME 197

CHAPTER 15. EVER AFTER 215

PREFACE

Lovely white swans drift effortlessly across the stunning pond, as reflective as a shiny new mirror. I draw closer while relishing the daisies cushioning my bare feet. The sun seems to compete for my attention as my head extends toward the warmth of the afternoon, much like the daisies reaching upward for growth. The fragrant smell of flowers is captivating and brings me to a halt. My joy overflows as I look down in admiration of the lovely white chiffon gown blowing rhythmically in sync with the wind. As I close my eyes, my head tilts slightly to focus on the direction of the familiar sound of an approaching horse and rider. Alas, I am convinced my charming Prince has arrived to whisk me away to Paradise…

"Get on out of here", mumbled the voice of one shoving me away as he zipped his pants and rolled over in bed. How could this be? How was I on the edge of Paradise and awakened to this nightmare? At six years old, I didn't know of something called dissociation, even though I had experienced it for at least a year now. My own father, no less. "I'm telling mother!" Why had I never said this before? Two years had passed since that night when I was yet 4 years old, and Daddy came in my room and took me to the kitchen and began 13 years of sexual abuse. Suddenly, he turned to a drawer and took out a revolver and pulled me close. He put the barrel to my head and swore to first kill my mother, and then me, if I ever breathed a word. He further declared I would ruin our family forever, and it would all be my fault. With another cruel shove, I was out of his room and running to mine. Tears were a way of letting something out that I couldn't say. I knew that from then on, I was subject to whatever he asked for the rest of my life. Soon the tears wore me down, and I drifted off to return once more to my field of daisies, and hoped to see the Prince on the white horse.

INTRODUCTION

"DADDY'S WORKIN' IN A COALMINE

GOIN' DOWN, DOWN, DOWN

WORKIN' IN A COALMINE

OOPS, ABOUT TO SLIP DOWN . . .

LORD, I'M SO TIRED . . .

HOW LONG CAN THIS GO ON?"

Recorded by Lee Dorsey 1966 / Songwriter: Allen Toussaint
Workin' In the Coal Mine Lyrics © Sony/ATV Music Publishing LLC

By the time the song, "Workin' In A Coalmine" was released, I was finally a teenager, and had been buried deep in the darkness of sexual secrets for over a decade. As a metaphor to the coalmines, I lived with black coal dust and ashes that failed to be cleansed with soap and water. The remains lodged deeper than one could ever see into themselves. Beneath the smiles and apropos behavior was a filthy, stained girl, that grew from a tainted child, and would bring the moldering slate into womanhood in just a few short years. With each attempt to reach within and believe for something more, the coal dust would attach itself to any efforts toward a wholesome and fulfilling existence. Black lung had analogously taken hold and was smothering any chance of breaking free.

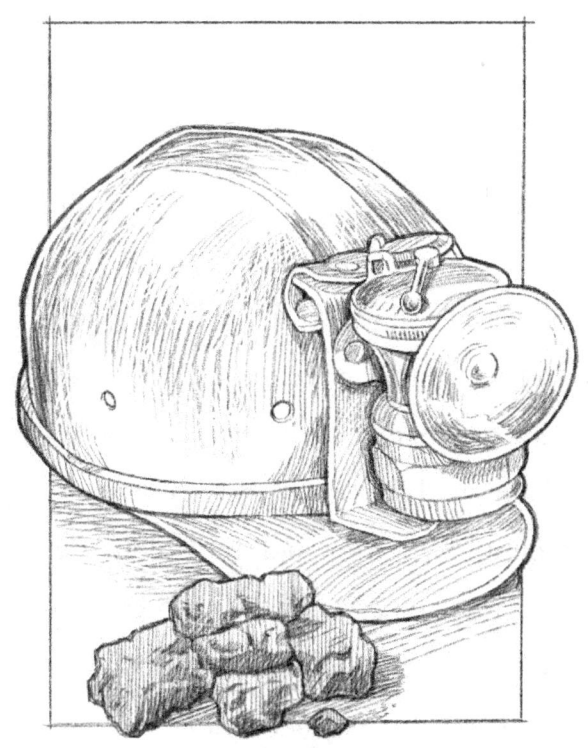

CHAP 1
COAL MINER'S DAUGHTER

"WELL A LOT OF THINGS HAVE CHANGED
   SINCE A WAY BACK THEN
AND IT'S SO GOOD TO BE BACK HOME AGAIN
NOT MUCH LEFT BUT THE FLOOR,
   NOTHING LIVES HERE ANYMORE
EXCEPT THE MEMORY OF A COAL MINER'S DAUGHTER"

Recorded by Loretta Lynn, 1970. Coal Miner's Daughter Lyrics © Sure - Fire Music Company

Every story must start somewhere . . . it may not be the moment of birth, but my beginning starts on a Saturday night, in the wee hours of the darkness when evil lurks and wandering thoughts take action. I have relived the event countless times, pondering what would have happened if only I had screamed out beyond the hand cupped over my mouth to silence me. The wall between my mother and me would become an impenetrable dark fortress to house secrets only known to my father and me. How could an almost four-year-old even know the difference between good and evil, right and wrong, appropriate and inappropriate? I had involuntarily enrolled in an accelerated learning experience that would tap into sexual awareness far before my time. Something was broken in that little child that night that would accompany a broken girl, and a broken woman. Appease me for a glimpse back to approximately 1956, in the coal-mining camp of Sayre, Alabama.

The backdrop of my life is unique itself and must be considered with regards to the flashbacks and snapshot memories for the years to come.

Sayre is an unincorporated coal-mining community 18 miles north of Birmingham, Alabama. I imagine the 1950's was the peak for Sayre, as most of the cookie cutter duplexes were occupied during those years. The coalminers' life was arduous and laboriously repetitive, with insufficient income for the needs of a family. Luxuries were reserved for the upper echelon of the world. Miners were paid in Company Scrip (a substitute for government-issued

I HAD INVOLUNTARILY ENROLLED IN AN ACCELERATED LEARNING EXPERIENCE THAT WOULD TAP INTO SEXUAL AWARENESS FAR BEFORE MY TIME.

legal tender or currency) called "Clacker". It could only be exchanged in Company Stores owned by the employer. These included a commissary, café, doctor and dentist. There was also a small bank, post office and school. Since most miners couldn't afford an automobile, life revolved around the mining camp. People came home after work, ate dinner, and congregated out in the yard or in the streets. The women would gather in late afternoons to gossip the latest trysts and discoveries from soap operas, as they watched their children at play. Teens walked around the camp listening to transistor radios playing the current hits. Most men would have a cold beer and play dominoes or various card games, such as Rook or Pinochle.

The top billboard tune was "Don't be Cruel", by none other than Elvis Presley. Elvis Presley first appeared on The Ed Sullivan Show September 9, 1956. Viewers got to see the full Elvis - legs, hips, and all - during the second segment, when he performed the up-tempo Little Richard song, 'Ready Teddy' and two verses of 'Hound Dog'. He was all the rage with the entire family. Everyone seemed to swoon over this "bad boy" with the innocent looking baby face. Without a doubt, the young hard-labor guys from the coalmines got a kick out of this country boy-turned-idol from Tupelo, Mississippi. Why, they were practically neighbors, and could identify with his roots of poverty and simplicity.

Nighttime television was mostly a family affair with shows such as I Love Lucy, Walt Disney's Wonderful World of Color (black and white for us), Lassie, Alfred Hitchcock, and the Red Skelton Show. The closest one could get to understanding the life in the coal mining camp is displayed in the movie, "Coalminer's Daughter". The Movie, released in 1980, stars Sissy Spacek, and is the life story of Country Hall of Fame's Loretta Lynn. She rose from abject poverty in the hills of Kentucky to becoming the most sought-after female country singer of her day. Interestingly, our lack of one thing, perhaps money and luxuries, gives way to focus on our God-given talents and abilities we may have never developed, had we been afforded the tangible things that can sometimes distract us from our destiny. Loretta Lynn and Elvis Presley are prime examples of destiny emerging from despair.

There's no question my father was a gifted and musically talented man. He played any and every instrument he ever held. (Spoken with no embellishment). There were numerous instruments in the community churches back in his youth, and he spent much of his free time moving from one instrument to another. Eventually, he could play them all. As a young lad, he ran away from home and joined a circus, playing the piano, harmonica, and guitar. He hitched rides on trains, thumbed on the open highways, and walked when there were no other options. His parents were ministers, and his father also worked full-time in the mines. His adventures away from the mining camp opened his eyes to thrills and a taste for drinking, drugs and the party life.

After returning home and getting back into school, he met my mother and they became involved at age 15 and 16. She ran away from home and married him and they were pregnant early on, but miscarried. Soon their first child, Michael, was born and I came along 22 months later. For my Daddy, something always seemed to be missing. He was inevitably the one to try something new first, be it dangerous or thrilling. He had five siblings, and always managed to be one step out in front of them. I don't remember much before three years old. I know Daddy was already drinking when I was three. Initially, his drinking was limited to the weekends. We soon learned to fear those 3 days from Friday afternoon until Sunday night. However, the weekends carried over to the weekdays, and soon his life was on a nefarious cycle heading down an inescapable dark mine of his own doing. Daddy and

Mother's relationship began and continued with physical and emotional abuse.

At any rate, let's return to that telling Saturday night on my father's lap. With one had cupped over my mouth, Daddy carried me to the kitchen. He sat me in his lap facing away from him and began to touch me and thrust himself against my back. I recall squirming my head from side to side, attempting to free my mouth. I felt as if I was going to sleep but couldn't help it. I now believe his hand was covering both my mouth and nose, and that I was slipping out of consciousness. His grip released momentarily as he whisked me around face to face. He gritted his teeth and squinted his eyes just like Mrs. Woodward's dog that was tied to a tree down the street from our house. His expression would be one I would see for the duration of our "Secret". The next thing I heard was my mother's name, "Pat! Get in here and fix me some breakfast. Janis is up walking around. Get her back in bed. What's she doing in here?" My pregnant mother got up and followed his orders. I headed to the bathroom and felt a burning sensation as I urinated. I whimpered and held myself when I got back in bed. After one "secret" encounter, I was terrified to answer my mother when she asked, "Are you alright?" I didn't want my Daddy to put me in his lap anymore.

My second brother, Steve, would be coming in five months. His life wouldn't be easy. The middle child has challenges of its own, but Steve would have learning issues that made it even harder to measure up to Daddy. Just before Steve's birth, my older brother, Michael, had this sensational dream about a sailor coming to visit my mother. Somehow the story got to my father, and he made accusations about Steve not being his son. At the age of four, I recall my parents arguing and my mother pleading with my father that it was only a dream. You can be sure my brother Michael got the first-degree interrogation on the story. Daddy had a way of turning statements around and asked Michael, "There was a sailor that came here and was with your Mama, wasn't there, boy? You better tell me." We were always afraid to say, "No". My Daddy would bring up that dream for many years to come.

Christmas was near and money was far away. In the early morning hours before dawn on the Sunday before Christmas, Daddy broke into the company bank across the street from our home. He was arrested and spent the holiday in jail. That Christmas, our grandmothers gave us each a present, and Santa left a sock nailed to the wall with a few pieces of hard candy, an orange, some unshelled nuts and a tangerine inside. We were thrilled with the gifts we received, and thankful Santa didn't leave coal in our sock. It is the first time I remember hearing that Santa would leave coal in your stocking if you were naughty, and I certainly felt naughty. Christmas passed, and baby Steve came a few weeks later in January of 1957. He cried a lot, and Mother seemed burdened with more than a new baby. Daddy would often stay out drinking until two or three in the morning. Late night arguments about money and a new baby resulted in a call to Daddy's uncle up North. There was a job opening for my Daddy's type of music in the Detroit area. The hopes were high to make more money in the club than he made working deep in the coal mines. As soon as Mother recovered from giving birth, she packed us up and we headed for Detroit, Michigan for a year. Everything we owned was given to us anyway, so there were no regrets. We rented a small furnished apartment. My brother Michael and I slept in the hallway on a twin cot.

Daddy landed the job playing the piano at a honkytonk. A "honkytonk" is defined as a cheap and disreputable bar that usually plays country music. My father played "honky-tonk" piano and seemed to fit into this environment. His style of music was a combination of Jerry Lee Lewis and

Floyd Cramer. The joint began to grow and was completely crowded on weekends. All the women flirted with, and took a liking to my Daddy, and he to them. Mother didn't like it much, but there was little she could do without ending up in a fight. Mother spent much of her time at home with two young children, and a new baby.

Summer ended and school would soon be starting. It was both a cultural and a temperature shock as well. We were complete southerners in a big northern city. A couple of days before school began, Mother walked us to the new school, and signed us up for the new year. The women in the office talked funny and they laughed at us when we talked back. I was entering first grade, and Michael third grade. I didn't like it, but then again, there were other things I didn't like that I couldn't do anything about. The next day, we took our sack lunches and found our way to school all by ourselves. We made it fine through school and found each other as planned when the bell rang that first day. We began walking down the sidewalk and couldn't figure out whether to turn left or right. We jotted back and forth, crossed through some yards, and ended up lost and roaming the streets in a bit of a panic. We had no phones in those days. Eventually, a policeman drove by and stopped. We froze in fear and held on to each other. We had seen a few policemen knocking on our door in the past. He approached us and asked where we lived. Neither of us knew the address, but we told him our Daddy played the piano and sang at Jay's honky-tonk. The officer took us there and sat us up on the bar. The bartender gave us a soda and some peanuts. Familiar music was playing in the background, and we started singing along. You see, our wonderful Aunt Kat, back in Alabama, had invested countless hours teaching Michael and me to sing both melody and harmony. The gift of music is one passed down to me from generations back.

The bartender and police officers seemed impressed that we could sing two-part harmony at 6 and 8 years old. The owner came out and verified that we were "Flippo's" children. Back at home, my father was hesitant when he saw flashing lights and heard a knock at the door. Daddy stayed in the back of the apartment and sent Mother to the door. It could have been regarding a fight Daddy had been involved in, a drug deal, something he had stolen, or just about anything. For Mother, it was a relief to see Michael and me sitting in the back seat of the patrol car. We would be seen sticking together for many years to come. As you are reading along, you may have an eye-opening moment yourself about your own dysfunctional upbringing. Don't let it escape you, as I am certain you will experience healing, if you won't push the opportunity away. Besides, we are moving back to the coalmining camp.

CHAP 2

ALABAMY BOUND

"JUST HEAR THAT CHOO-CHOO SOUND,

I KNOW THAT SOON WE'RE GONNA COVER GROUND,

AND THEN I'LL HOLLER SO

THE WORLD WILL KNOW,

HERE I GO!

I'M ALABAMY BOUND!"

Popularized by Al Jolson, and recorded by Blossom Seeley (1925). Written in 1924, with music by Ray Henderson, words by Buddy DeSylva and Bud Green

Detroit was short lived, and we were Alabama bound once again. It so happened that the same duplex we had previously occupied was vacant, and my parents took it back. As we entered through the back door, I had an intrusive memory of that first night in the kitchen, but it was as though I was standing at the door observing from behind. I could see my father behind me and what he was doing, hear him unzip his pants, and feel the evil in the atmosphere. It was my first experience with flashbacks. I also remember beginning to sit with my dresses tucked tightly underneath my legs, and my legs shut together. It shouldn't be a consuming thought for a young girl of six. I always felt my father was watching me every chance he could. I felt dirty and ashamed of the events occurring between my father and me, but I couldn't risk our lives to bring it out into the open.

My nightly "Now I lay me down to sleep" prayers became longer that year. It was partly due to my Sunday School teacher. She told us that Jesus loved little children all over the world, and He would listen to us when we pray. Our parents had no interest in church or the things of God in those years, but passion couldn't be higher for Michael and me. Just two years prior, when I was about to turn 4, Michael and I had walked across the back yard to a small Pentecostal Church of God. During the message, the minister talked about Jesus being a friend that would never leave you, and one that would always love you. He asked anyone to come forward that wanted a friend. I clomped down the aisle and knelt at an old wooden altar. I squeezed my eyes shut and peeked out from side to side. I was seeking attention and approval. I could hear a lady singing "Into my heart, into my heart, come into my heart, Lord Jesus. Come in today, come in to stay. Come into my heart, Lord Jesus". A few older women, with tight buns on top of their head, began to lay hands on my head and shoulders. I was following their suggestions by asking Jesus to come into my heart and suddenly felt a bonding and an association with my Creator. I began to cry. This Friend really did what the minister said he would do. They told me I was SAVED, and the whole church lined up and shook my hand. I didn't really understand much else, but I was happy to have a friend that would always be with me.

From then on, Michael and I walked to church on every occasion (there were 3 churches in the coal mining camp), begged a ride with anyone that would take us, and cried when we couldn't go. Church and singing were all we lived for, and we were very good at it. Since we had returned from Detroit, we had no furniture in our living room, but Daddy had horse-traded around, and we had two pianos instead! Michael would play on one and I the other. Our uncle Bill and aunt Kat, (Daddy's younger sister) lived in the camp as well, and always let us hang out in the summer. She's the same aunt who spent hours standing at the ironing board teaching Michael and me to sing. My Daddy picked up early on that he could make extra money booking us in churches singing gospel music, and soon we were singing in various cities throughout the state every weekend. As soon as we walked off stage, Daddy went out the side door to smoke and drink. At the time, it was just a gig for the money. We were so popular that we made a 45 record and sold them at our events. Daddy was already a regular singer and musician on the Country Boy Eddie show, a weekly morning television program in Birmingham. When Country Boy Eddie found out we could sing, we accompanied Daddy on the weekends. To outsiders, our family seemed great, but we all know looks somewhat resemble gift wrapping. You can't imagine what's inside until you take the outer wrapping off.

I am grateful for my Daddy's parents, looking back. They would allow my brother and me to spend Saturday nights twice each month. We were awakened sharply at 5 a.m. Sunday morning, and quickly dressed for church and headed to the car for a long drive to Birmingham. My grandparents, ordained ministers, oversaw a Sunday morning service in the Veteran's hospital. When the service concluded, we walked from room to room singing and praying for the bedridden patients. On our drive back to my grandparents' church, we made a regular stop for a donut and juice. Twice each month we visited nursing homes on Thursday evenings hoping to bring some cheer to many of the residents, who had no friends or family. Two Saturdays a month, we went to the local jail, and the state prison in Montgomery, Alabama for church services with the inmates. I learned at a very young age of the suffering and pain others felt from those visits to the veteran's hospitals, nursing homes, jails, and prisons. It was a glorious break from the stress and tension of our home life. Although, I often worried about mother and our little brother when we were away. We had no way to contact one another once we left home. Our middle brother, Steve, was still a toddler, and Daddy didn't pay much attention to him yet. Daddy would bring "drinking buddies" home frequently at 3 a.m., and have mother cook a full country breakfast. It wasn't unusual to find strangers sleeping on our couch or in the floor the morning after. One Sunday after church Daddy and his friends were in the living room drinking. They were laughing about Daddy having given baby Steve beer to drink. He was beginning to wobble and fall. Daddy had placed a row of quarters on the floor and asked Steve to pick them up. They roared with laughter as Steve staggered across the room trying to walk toward the quarters. I felt sorry for Steve but was too afraid to speak up.

It was now more than a year of Daddy coming into my room since moving back to the coal mining camp. I could practically sense the restlessness stirring in him and tried to gear myself up for what was to come. It seemed to be a warning or a preparation. This one balmy night, Daddy stumbled in the house, as usual in a drunken stupor. I recall his clammy hands, stained with coal, the smell of liquor mixed with Camel cigarettes, and his blue eyes completely lined with black from working in the mines. His intentions were interrupted by a vicious scream from outside our duplex. It was around 4 in the morning and our neighbor, Mrs. "H", was screaming at Mr. H, "I've had just about enough of your cheating, lying, and drinking".

(great emphasis on each word) Their argument escalated and ensued to the front porch. We were going out to see what was happening just in time to observe her thrusting a butcher knife right into his stomach. Bowed forward and grasping the knife's handle as he pushed her hand away, he stumbled down the stairs and onto the ground as he begged God for his life. By now, a group dressed in nightgowns, pink sponge hair curlers, housecoats, shortie pajamas, and an array of sleeping attire, had congregated in the yard of Mrs. H. Soon the sounds of sirens blasted through the darkness as both ambulance and police arrived on the scene. Everyone knew their story, as they were the objects of much gossip, and no one knew ours. Theirs was out in the open and ours was secluded behind doors. I remember wishing my father were that man. Why couldn't my mother say she had enough and rescue us all from physical, emotional, and my sexual abuse?

Daddy had whetted his appetite for the nightlife during our year in Detroit. It was a way to feel important and somewhat of a star. For boredom's sake and finances, Daddy began playing music every night possible, worked the hoot owl shift in the mines (11pm-7am) and slept all day. When the shifts changed at the mines, the men would all walk home carrying their two-tiered lunch buckets. The pails were round, with a base of about 9", and approximately a foot tall. The bottom layer was for ice, and the top contained their lunch. They each carried a large thermos filled with coffee. Atop their heads sat a protective helmet with a large light in front. The mine was dark, cavernous, and lonely. You would often hear of miners being trapped, injured, and some even crushed or smothered to death. Everyone lived with a sense of caution day by day. Daddy had more reason than some to fear the mine. His father was in a mining accident when Daddy was just a lad, and was completely crushed, and told he would not live. The family was messaged to go to the hospital to say their goodbyes. They all stood around the bed and mourned the lifeless body of my grandfather. When visiting hours concluded, they all were instructed to leave. They had no form of communication with the hospital. During the night, my grandfather was visited by an angel of the Lord that spoke to him and instructed him to get out of bed and be healed. Being a man of unwavering faith, he stood to his feet and began to shout and declare, "I am healed, I am healed". The hospital orderly came and tried to restrain him in fear that he had gone insane. They called for the doctors and nurses. They all came and witnessed an absolute miracle. His story was printed into thousands of leaflets that were dropped from airplanes over communities in the southeast as a testimony that miracles still happen. I have included a copy of the tract.

Early one morning, Daddy came home from working all night in the mines. Daddy had begun mixing alcohol and drugs to keep up the pace of two jobs. He would take something to help him sleep, and something to stimulate him in the waking hours. As a result, Daddy was either gone or sleeping. Mother was left to discipline us children. When we disobeyed, our punishment was to be placed in the room where my father was sleeping. We had to stay for 30 minutes. The room was a darkened dungeon, with blinds and dark curtain, so my father could sleep during the day. I always prayed he would be snoring, so I would be safe. Any type of movement on my part would stir him awake and he would peek out of one eye to see which child was in the room. I sat against the wall with my knees drawn and my head buried. I was trying to be invisible. I dreaded and feared those moments, and to think my mother put me there. If only she knew, she would never hand me over to him. It felt as if I were being cast into a lion's den. The lion was waiting for the prey, and it happened to be me.

Children were only allowed in the house to eat, sleep, or use the bathroom. It was nothing to be missing for 3 or

4 hours at a time. Children just roamed around the community, trying to pass the time away. Our house had no air-conditioning in the summer, and a coal-driven heater in the living room for the winter. Mother managed to make lots of Kool-Aid pops in the ice trays to cool us down in the summertime. Occasionally, she would throw the hose pipe over the clothesline and let us run back and forth through the water. Food was not abundant and consisted of biscuits and gravy for breakfast, crackers and peanut butter for lunch, beans, cornbread and fried potatoes for dinner. Greens were my mother's favorite. I would go hunting for these wild greens called Poke Sallet.

One afternoon in the spring of 1959 I wanted to surprise my mother with a batch. I ventured to the end of the road and went down the side of a hill. I didn't realize I was butted up against the fiery embers burning from the slate dump. In a coalmining camp, the coal companies would haul off slate (generally, unusable pieces of coal) to different places throughout the community. Over time, the weight of the materials created pressure in the earth and resulted in spontaneous combustion, deep within the dump. It would burn until all the combustible material was burned up. This could take years. While the coal in the dump was burning, the slate and rocks wouldn't burn, but resulted in a smoldering effect that would turn red. I spotted some poke sallet just a few steps from where I was standing and suddenly my feet began to sink and the heat from the smoldering ashes began to surround me. I screamed, "Help! Help, somebody help me!" Out of nowhere appeared a young teenage boy wearing only a pair of swimming trunks. He was sunbathing in preparation for his night at the Prom. With no hesitation, he ran directly toward me, sank in the ash as he lifted me out and we ran for safety. We were both screaming, but his scream intensified beyond mine. When we got to the grass, I looked down and his feet were melted together from the smoldering ashes. He had risked his life to save mine. The ambulance eventually arrived and took him into the city, where he was kept in the hospital for a few days, while his severe burn wounds were treated. My mother took me to the hospital to visit him and to give him a small bouquet of flowers. There is an article I still have from the front page of the Birmingham News, praising his bravery and heroism. When I returned from the hospital, my father was drinking and just looked at me and said, "You think you're something, don't you?"

A psychologist by the name of Erik Erikson released his theory of Psychosocial Development in 1959. He developed a theory of development based on our psychosocial interactions in life, with eight stages offering an opportunity for one of two outcomes.

STAGE 1: TRUST VS. MISTRUST (BIRTH-18 MONTHS)

He saw the first year of a child's life as either being nurtured and having attentive needs met or being deprived of the care and attention needed during this stage. With proper care and attention, the child would develop trust that would determine whether the child would trust others throughout life. For the neglected child, the resulting deprivation would leave the child having mistrust. His theory was that personality is set up in a predetermined order and builds on each previous stage. This is referred to as the Epigenetic Principle. So then, Erikson puts a high premium on having this initial stage of development end with positive trust. Each of Erikson's stages come with a virtue. The "trust vs. mistrust" virtue results in either hope or hopelessness.

STAGE 2: AUTONOMY VS. SHAME AND DOUBT (18 MONTH - 3 YEARS)

This stage gives opportunity for the child to exercise independence and explore boundaries and limits. Parents are encouraged to allow their child to branch out and begin to make some choices, while the parents are balancing the limits in a safe environment. The resulting life quality is "autonomy". The overbearing or neglecting parent risks the possibility of "autonomy', and "shame" is the inevitable outcome. As a result, the child will lack self-esteem, and feel a sense of shame or doubt in their choices and abilities, according to Erikson. The virtue associated with this stage is "Will".

STAGE 3: INITIATIVE VS. GUILT (AGES 3-6 YEARS)

Erikson's third stage of development is the time children begin to assert themselves and take initiative. It is a time to role play and explore their interpersonal relationships with other children. These should be the years when children ask lots of questions about themselves, others, their sexuality, and differences. The resulting virtue acquired during this stage is "Purpose".

This is where we have landed. As we exit Erikson's theory to consider thus far, my M.O. (modus operandi) is rooted in mistrust, shame, and guilt. At the delicate age of 6, I could have transitioned through the first three of Erikson's stages of development with complete trust, autonomy and initiative. Instead, my trust was compromised, and in the place of any feelings of autonomy, I was shame-filled, manipulated and controlled, and doubted myself. My broken child was becoming a girl, with no confidence to initiate. I was deprived of my purpose, and felt it was intertwined with my father's choices about me. Constantly ravaged with fear and anxiety at nighttime, I began to suck my thumb, bite my nails, and twist my hair. I was dealing with the pressure from the outside in, rather than vocalizing and bringing my fears out in the open. With no liberty to externalize, I survived with an unhealthy internalization. During that same year, I experienced my first encounter with dissociation.

The weight for a six-year-old should have been learning my ABC's, spelling 3-5 letter words, and playing "London Bridge". Instead, the weight of doing the right thing, saying just enough, and daring not to say what is forbidden pressed upon me. Perhaps it was the whole Eriksonian "initiative" thing at work, but one afternoon in my father's bed, I recall attempting to exercise some initiative. The room was stuffy, and the curtains were drawn. A window fan was moving the hot air from the bedroom to the heat of the moment. He held me down and I cleared my throat and mumbled, "I'm telling

Mama". "What did you just say girl"? "I'm telling on you", said I with less confidence than before." He gripped a much tighter hold on my thigh and reached across the bed to a nightstand. He reached for the knob of the old wooden drawer that had to be rocked up and down to open, and suddenly his hand was holding a gun I had never seen before. I had heard him bragging about what he would do with it on occasion, but now he was pointing it at me. "If you EVER tell your

AS SURELY AS THE COLD BARREL OF THE GUN TREMBLED AGAINST MY CURLY HAIR COVERING MY TEMPLE, A CHILL STRUCK THROUGH MY BODY WITH A MESSAGE THAT I, A CHILD, HELD THE FUTURE OF MY MOTHER, MYSELF, AND MY FATHER ON MY SHOULDERS.

Mama about this, I will kill her AND you." As surely as the cold barrel of the gun trembled against my curly hair covering my temple, a chill struck through my body with a message that I, a child, held the future of my mother, myself, and my father on my shoulders. I acquired the sensation of a golf ball-sized lump in my throat that could not be swallowed away. It would remain throughout my life when I felt stressed and overwhelmed.

Abuse, sickness, and suffering are difficult to understand and to interpret. We would love to think we could explain the evil and suffering in our world. There was a father in the New Testament, whose name we aren't told, who had a son with severe seizures from birth. They were so extreme that he convulsed and threw himself into fires, rocks, and was constantly bruised and suffering from his maladies. That father came to Jesus in Mark chapter nine and said, "If you can do anything for my son, help us. Jesus replied, "If you can believe, all things are possible." Did they all wait for some lightning to strike from heaven? Perhaps some fire would shoot forth from the fingertips of this man Jesus. The audacious father cried through his tears and said, "Lord, I believe; help me with the unbelief part." Jesus stood in front of the boy and said, "Thou dumb and deaf spirit, I charge thee, come out of him and enter no more into him." The boy lay as if dead. Jesus reached and took him by the hand and lifted him up; and he arose. He was made completely whole that very moment from then on.

Each of us arrive at a despairing chapter of life such as I experienced that life-threatening day at the slate dump. We feel hopeless and cry out for someone to save us. I felt as if I were screaming into an abyss at the edge of the universe with no chance of a response. Raymond Burrell jumped in and risked his life for mine that day. I would have perished without him. I surrendered to my rescuer, and my life was spared. He bears the scars to this day. There is always One available to lift us from the ashes that would destroy us. Jesus Christ is available right here and right now. He was willing to jump in and give His life in place of yours. Would you consider taking a leap of faith and inviting the Friend, Jesus, to come and live in your heart? Speaking of jumping in, we are going down to the River . . .

CHAP 3
THE RIVER

"SHALL WE GATHER AT THE RIVER
THE BEAUTIFUL, THE
   BEAUTIFUL, RIVER
GATHER WITH THE SAINTS
   AT THE RIVER
THAT FLOWS BY THE
   THRONE OF GOD."

Written in 1864 by American poet and gospel music composer, Robert Lowry. Public Domain.

The River and I have always gone 'round and about. However, as experiences vary from person to person, an external view of a thing doesn't always reveal the truth that might lie within it. A fresh coat of paint prevents one from seeing the previous layer, or even the old wallpaper that is hidden beneath. To borrow a thought from "A Tale of Two Cities", the river holds the best of times and the worst of times for me. There is a program on television about river monsters wherein the stars of the show seek out these monsters lurking deep in the dark waters. It is always an unexpected moment when these river monsters furiously break the waters and reveal their insatiable desire to conquer the enemy.

My issues with the river began at the age of 2 1/2 years old. Our family would periodically gather at the river with my aunts, uncles, and grandparents for picnics and games. The men would go off fishing and exploring while the women spread out the blankets and unloaded the food. My grandparents would build a fire and fry up the fish on the riverbank. There was always sweet tea for the grown-ups and Kool-Aid for the children. On this unforgettable occasion, my brother Michael and I wandered off from the water's edge and stumbled beneath the surface. From the moment my aunt first noticed we were missing, she insisted we were missing 5 full minutes. Everyone above the surface was scrambling hysterically and searching the woods with no success. My grandmother, whom I never saw wear anything but a dress, waded into the waters, and began praying fervently out loud. Her hands were extended beneath the surface, combing from side to side, and miraculously grabbed onto my brother Michael, not knowing I was hanging on to his hand. They all declared that day a miracle!

Over the next few years, we visited the river often, as it provided our only source of protein. Daddy hunted 3 or 4 times each week and brought home deer, squirrel, rabbit, birds and other such animals. (Bambi, Chip n' Dale, Daffy, and Tweety Bird, I'm sorry) Shortly following my 7th birthday, Daddy piled a bunch of kids from the camp (coal mining community where we lived) and took us down to the river. He had been drinking that day, and my mother didn't want to go along. We were all 10 years and under. Again, I always wore dresses, and this day was no different. I didn't know how to swim and stayed close to the water's shallow edges.

My horrendous fears of something over my head had developed at two years of age, after tumbling down a flight of stairs which resulted in a two inch "L- shaped" gash atop my head. I was taken to the emergency room in Port Huron, Michigan, and vividly recall my mother running out of the bathroom naked and scooping me up. She grabbed a robe and screamed for help. We lived upstairs in two rooms and had to share a bathroom with the owners. Mother's scream got the attention of the owners and they offered to drive us to the emergency room. I recall feeling the blood oozing from atop my head as mother held me with one hand and put pressure on the gash with a white towel. Upon arrival, the nurses peeled me from my mothers' arms, laid me on a gurney, and held me down (one nurse on each side). As they wheeled me into the surgery room, they covered my whole body with a sheet and only left my wound exposed for suturing. I screamed and screamed, "I can't see my feet. . . . I can't see my feet". From then on, I panicked if someone tried to hold me down or cover something over my head.

Perhaps the fear of water over my head and my father's forceful grip culminated in unbearable anxiety for a child of 7 years. My father, while still underwater, had swum from the depth of the river and grabbed my legs out from under me. Out of sheer panic, I frantically clung to him. My sheer fright from that day in the emergency room grew when combined with the muddy waters covering my head that prevented me from seeing. It was as if a massive river monster had me in its jaws and was wrestling me until I surrendered. Right there, with children swimming and playing all around us, Daddy began to touch me and rub against me. I felt his finger penetrate me for the first time. I moaned, "Ouch", and he squeezed tighter on my stomach. When he finished, he tossed me over his head, swam away, and I plunged into the depths of despair and deep waters. I had no forewarning to catch a deep breath and I began to descend into the blurry abyss with no skills for survival. My feet touched the floor of the river and I pushed and floated through the murky waters, which I had seen years before at the river, and I finally surfaced to catch a breath. My father had returned to the bank and began laughing and telling me to swim or drown. My friends were telling me to "dog- paddle", which to my fretful heart, seemed to work. As I felt my feet on the bottom, I slowly dragged myself to the bank. It was reminiscent of a dream in slow motion, dauntingly attempting to escape with no success. My father was clapping his hands and saying, "now you can swim". I dared not show my true feelings, because if they all began to spill out now, the river would surely overflow. In my masking manner, I pretended to laugh along.

In a study by the National Scientific Council on the Developing Child, they state, "when young children experience serious fear- triggering events, they learn to associate that fear with the context and conditions that accompanied it. In psychological terms, a process called, "Fear-Conditioning" occurs when two stimuli are paired, one of which would not usually elicit a negative emotional response. Over time, the relation between the two stimuli generalizes a fear response to other neutral stimuli that have characteristics resembling the negative stimulus. What is known as "Generalization" results. Generalization, in my case, could be all male authority figures, all miners, all men who smoke, all men who are drinking, etc. Another generalization from these few accounts could include, rivers, feeling dominated and restrained, having one's head covered, etc.

Within weeks of that daunting river episode, my baby brother, Dirk was born. I had just turned 8 years old the week before. He was the light of my father's life. My parents were only 28 and 27 at the time. They had four children 10 and under. I remember one stormy afternoon when Dirk was only 3 ½ weeks old. My father had been gone the whole weekend drinking with friends. We were out of food and supplies for baby Dirk and mother decided to drive to a grocery store four or five miles away. She left us to watch over baby Dirk. As she approached the old rickety one-way bridge over the Warrior River the car began to slide. The bridge had wooden planks that rose above the main floor to provide as a guide, and possibly for additional support. There were no seat belts at that time and I'm certain the tires were lacking any traction. She heard a voice from heaven say, "Pat, let go of the wheel and lay down in the front seat and cross your arms." With no hesitation and with no time to spare, she obeyed the voice. Seconds later, the car crashed through the railing of the bridge and bolted over and over, landing upside down between the river and the bank. With broken ribs, bruises, and cuts, she crawled from the car and up an embankment to safety. With no communication available in those days, hours later our mother arrived with strangers who offered her a ride after witnessing someone climbing up the cliff of the river, struggling and bloody.

On many other occasions, there was a secluded place on the river that was delegated for lovers and "necking" in the evening. As soon and my father came home from work, which was about 3:30 every afternoon, he would find an excuse to leave the house. He made me wait down the street, as if I was out playing, and he would pick me up and drive to the river, or up the knoll known as Burr Hill. He often had beer in the car, and the combination of beer, smoke and coal shavings was nauseating. When drinking, he was careless and angry. He wasn't the wimpy type you see in movies that smiles and offers candy and treats to trick children. He would firmly say, "Get over here!" Sometimes I would speak through my tears and try to plead, "Daddy, please . . . . No Daddy". I didn't try that too much when I could smell the liquor, because I was so afraid of him. So, with my heart racing and my palms sweaty, I crawled up into his lap. It was almost a ritual. It was reminiscent of the first night in the kitchen each time. Now that I was almost 9, I could feel my body beginning to change. I suppose you could say I was prepubescent. My developing body was tender to touch, and he would caress me as if I were fully developed. It would be 40 years later, when I became certified as a sexologist, that I would realize he had many indicators of a pedophile. According to the literature from the 1960's, a pedophile was described with this criterion:

a. The act or fantasy of engaging in sexual activity with prepubertal children is a repeatedly preferred or exclusive method of achieving sexual excitement.

b. If the individual is an adult, the prepubertal children are at least ten years younger than the individual. If the individual is a late adolescent, no precise age difference is required, and clinical judgment must consider the age difference as well as the sexual maturity of the child.

When he finished that day, he kept me in his lap and said, "you can drive the car home". I was still zoned out in my secret place of daisies and swans when he yelled, "look out . . . . you're going in the ditch!". I snapped back to realize I was the only one with hands on the wheel. He laughed out loud and continued directing me for the next 3 or 4 miles, until we ended up in the driveway behind the house. My mother came out the back door and said, "Lord Curtis, what are you doing letting her drive that car? She's not even 9. Janis, you get in here and set the table". He replied, "I'll do what I want and there's nothing you can do about it." She was holding a spatula in one hand, and he walked over and slapped her on the butt, and they started jesting and laughing. From then on, his excuse was that he was taking me to drive.

I began noticing my father constantly joking around with other young girls, who seemed to crave the attention. Somehow, they always ended up hanging around him, or sitting on his shoulders, or doing flips and summersaults for him. Was I the only one aware of the way he seemed to zone in on every detail of their body? I felt responsible to become a watchdog over the friends and family of the female sort. Surely, he wouldn't do anything to them. It was so much pressure that I tried to shift any playtime or games away from my home. It was a "Danger" zone. Forty-five years later I would hear a sorrowful story from a woman who knew my father when he was 18. She was only 5, but she told me he molested her one time and that she was so ashamed that she threw her panties under the front porch and hid them in the dirt. She cried on my shoulder and my heart ached wondering how many others shared our story over the years. Unfortunately, there would be at least 5 more women that approached me after I began telling my story.

In the summer of 1961, my church had a baptism service at that same river. We would always sing, "Shall we gather at the river" as the candidates lined up and made a procession into the water. I took my place in line, thinking of the scary events that had occurred beneath the water's calm appearance. My heart pounded and I felt it vibrate in the water as we all held hands and moved closer to the pastor who was beckoning us to come closer. My silent prayer was that a cleansing would bathe away all the filth and evil associated with the river. As I went down, it seemed I would never surface again. I couldn't concentrate on the holiness of the moment. I feared the pastor having control and pushing me under and just when I thought there was no breath left, he pulled

> **I WAS LEARNING TO LIVE ON THE OUTSIDE WHILE DYING ON THE INSIDE, AS I SHIVERED IN THE COLD BREEZES FROM THE RIVER.**

me up from the power of the waters beneath. I pretended to be so happy, but I realized something was deeply different about me that day. Others were crying in joyfulness as they emerged from the river. I was crying uncontrollably and momentarily felt a sense of community and belonging with the other baptismal candidates. I quickly felt vulnerable and painted on a smile and started singing and clapping my hands. I was learning to live on the outside while dying on the inside, as I shivered in the cold breezes from the river.

In the previous chapter, we discussed Erickson's psychosocial stages of development from birth to school age. We have now arrived at the next stage, which is: Industry vs. Inferiority. This occurs from ages 6-12. According to Erickson, with proper caretakers and the appropriate environment, this stage develops our sense of "Industry", rather than inferiority. Industry brings out one's self- competence, self-concept, and confidence in being able to organize and make decisions. Without the proper nurturing and care, inferiority is the result. Inferiority is the condition of being lower in status or quality than others. The first three children in our family struggled greatly with inferiority. I can't say it is foreigner to me at times, to this day. It was indeed a challenge to our self-esteem to hear our mother constantly berated, while also being told we were worthless and no good. The physical abuse began to escalate in our home. Mother could expect to be struck, slapped, kicked or shoved for no apparent reason. The spankings we once received became whippings that left belt and buckle marks for a couple of days. My oldest brother and I began to try to defend our mother from being struck. While we thought we were assisting, we were merely agitating the violence. There must have been something gargantuan troubling my father from his own childhood; something that he possibly had never told another.

There is an intriguing story in the Bible about the river. In II King 5, there was a famous captain of the host of the King of Syria. By him, God had given deliverance to the whole nation of Syria. Just as in our day, disease doesn't pass over the mighty, the rich, the famous, or anyone. Captain Naaman was diagnosed with Leprosy. One of the young women taken captive by Captain Naaman, became the servant to Naaman's wife. She told Naaman's wife, "If your husband could go see the prophet Elisha (in Israel), he could get healed of this leprosy. With no hesitation, the King of Syria sent the King of Israel $80,000 in gold and silver, along with ten changes of the finest apparel (designer specials) of the day. When Elisha the prophet heard the King of Israel was in distress, he suggested the King send Naaman to him. So Naaman arrived at the dwelling of Elisha with his chariot, horses, and his servant. Elisha sent his messenger to Naaman with the message, "Go and wash in Jordan seven times, and your flesh will be clean." Captain Naaman wasn't used to being instructed by servants, and especially ones that told him to dip in the filthy river seven times. So, he left and said, "I thought this prophet would step out, say some big prayers to God, perhaps strike his hand over me, and I would be healed." Naaman was also prejudice about that particular river because it was in Israel. He preferred the rivers of Damascus, his homeland. As he was departing, his servant said, "Captain, if this prophet had told you to do some great thing to be healed, wouldn't you have done it? Think about it, he only asked you to dip seven times." Still frustrated and angry, Naaman stubbornly began to dip. Can you imagine dip number 3 or 4? He was probably thinking, "This is the dumbest thing I have ever done in my life. Wait until they hear about this back at home." Still nothing at dip 5 or 6. Maybe he was even starting to walk back to the bank, but he dipped that seventh time and something supernatural began to surge though his body, and he ascended out of the water with the skin of a baby. He came before the prophet Elisha and said, "Behold, now I know that there is no God in all the earth; but in Israel."

Captain Naaman was a great and noble man by some standards. He was lacking in the spiritual arena altogether. As many often do, he couldn't grasp the simplicity of God's love. He imagined great demonstrations and displays in elaborate fashion concerning Almighty God. God instead showed Himself in something very doable. Naaman had issues receiving and felt he should do something magnificent to earn this healing. His first test was feeling entitled to see the prophet for himself. We sometimes buy in to thinking if we can contact a specific speaker, famous pastor, or faith healer that our miracle can come. We can't comprehend that humbling ourselves to dip seven times in a river is all we need to do to exercise our faith. The word for Naaman was to dip seven times in the river. Naaman's part was to act on the word. "Faith without works is dead" (James 2:17). God is always willing to do His part, and he wants us to always be willing to do ours.

Would you consider taking your own leap of faith? What is your malady or illness this very moment? If you feel as though you are drowning in the river of despair, take heart. Immerse yourself in the love of Jesus and let the healing waters cleanse you of all troubles and doubt. Naaman represents you and me, covered with filth and sin. We are offered a simple solution to a death sentence. Wash in the river of love and be cleansed, forgiven, and free. "But it seems too easy", we might say. So much had been stolen from us. Could we ever take it back? Have you ever been "forayed?" I have. Keep reading.

*(DSM_III displus.sk/DSM/subory/dsm. 3.pdf) DSM-III

CHAP 4
FORAYED

"WHO WILL CRY FOR THE LITTLE GIRL
I DON'T THINK THAT YOU CAN SAVE ME
WHO WILL CRY FOR THE LITTLE GIRL
WILL SOMEONE PLEASE COME AND SAVE ME!?"

Who Will Cry? (For the Little Girl), Written and performed by Schawayna Raie, 2017

The word foray means a sudden attack with intention to ravage or pillage. Other synonyms include torment, disturb, rattle one's cage, bother. Those in the military are familiar with the word with regards to foraying into the enemy territory. Somehow the word seems appropriate from my perspective. I was pillaged and suddenly disturbed from my innocence and purity far before my time. I truly hadn't considered the long-term effects of my sexual abuse until my body began responding to adolescence. My dissociating of a prince coming to rescue me was clouded with doubts that a prince would specifically select me from all the other princesses in the land. Although, my dissociating never included anyone other than myself, and an unrevealed person on a glistening white horse.

I was well into the Piaget's concrete operational stage of development, which covers ages 7-11, as well as Erik Erikson's psychosocial stage of Industry vs. Inferiority, ages 6-12. Piaget was a psychologist that proposed four stages of cognitive development over a lifetime. The first of Piaget's cognitive stages occurs from birth-2 years. It is the sensorimotor stage, and consists of connecting experiences with vision, hearing, as well as interactions with objects (stepping, sucking, gripping). Toddlers experience object permanence during this stage. The second stage from Piaget is the pre-operational stage and includes ages 2-7. Symbolic thought is the outcome of this stage, which is a type of thought where a word or an object can represent some other thing. This is when a child uses pretend play, drawing, writing, and acting.

Back to the Piaget's Concrete Operational stage and myself. At this stage of development, a child should be able to have organized and rationale thinking. In addition, this stage allows inductive thinking, which involves drawing inferences from observations to make a generalization from them. I felt this part of Piaget's theory working during these years. I could generalize from previous observations. Unfortunately, it led to believing I would never escape my situation. However, due to the extreme dysfunctionality of my home environment, being rational and organized was offshore and beyond my reach. These concepts require a proper atmosphere to thrive and allow for expression and testing grounds. This stage of development left me disturbed hearing other girls boast phrases such as, "I'm Daddy's little girl". It sounded unfit and inappropriate. I wondered if they were doing the same things we were doing when they said it? I was conflicted with both empathy and loathing for my father. My Christian faith always encouraged us to pray for our family members, especially those who needed salvation. My prayer life was very selfish and always seemed to wish my father was out of the way. I would crumble in tears and beg God to forgive my thoughts. I always remembered the Bible verse that said God's ways are higher than my ways, and His thoughts are higher than mine. I sometimes wondered if God accepted me with the types of prayers I would pray, and the questions I would ask of Him. My maturing brain was now able to process, to some degree, and planning for the future; well, it just brought planning the future to a halt.

The Spring of 1963 brought a dreadful day that would reveal a broken girl in a new light. Every Spring, our circuit of churches gathered for a big District Convention in Bessemer, Alabama. Michael and I were representing our region and scheduled to sing. I was thrilled to attend and be part of anything to do with church. It was such a release for me. I wore a white dress that my grandmother had made from a flour sack. I felt fresh and clean. I sneaked out during the sermon to walk around and have a soda before our part on the program. Church was the only place I could ever go where my Father would not be found. My brother, Michael, wore his regular old sports coat with sleeves closer to his elbows than his wrists. We both had our "performance outfit" for the TV show on Saturdays and the singings on the weekends. A strange lady walked up to me and whispered, "Honey, I think you better go to the bathroom; you have blood on the back of your dress." Clueless as to what was happening, my body was experiencing some new sensations, but I ignored the signs. With no time to visit the bathroom, I quickly asked my brother if I could wear his coat over my dress. He handed it to me, and we walked right up on stage and sang our duet. That's how I first found out about menstruation. I managed to keep it a secret for the rest of 5th grade. After all, I was getting great at keeping secrets. So many to keep. . . .

I was just out of 5th grade and about to turn 11 years old. I had been menstruating for about 4 months currently, and my mother didn't even know. I was completely uneducated about my body, and I thought the blood was coming from something my father was doing, and so I kept it to myself. I would feel premenstrual pains every month, and I thought I had a disease or that I could die. I would just say I was sick at my stomach, which was a common complaint of mine growing up. It was my attempt at crying out but unfortunately, no one was listening. Among the strict Pentecostal community I associated with in those days, there was no talk of our bodies, and certainly mentioning words such as "pregnant" was not allowed. I was slapped in the face once by an older woman in the church for saying a girl was "pregnant". Looking back, anything sexual was referred to as "playing ugly", "got in trouble" (pregnant), "on the rag", or having the curse.

That Summer my grandparents were the talk of the town in a new Mercury Monterey Breezeway. The unique feature of the car included a slanted rear window that was electric. There were hardly any cars at that time with air conditioning (approximately 35%), and I was thrilled when they asked my brother and me to go on a trip with them to the Midwest. I was ecstatic to meet my distant cousins and to escape my situation for a week. However, at the last minute my father decided to go along. Looking back, I possessed a mind-boggling ability to seamlessly switch from hopelessness to bliss. Dissociation and reality somehow merged into a middle ground that doesn't have a clinical name. Perhaps I never really understood how to be genuine and authentic. It was a much simpler task to dissociate than to dwell on the truth. How could I possibly confront actual reality? I embraced dissociating as a comforting, coping mechanism.

The trip itself was rather non-eventful. My brother and I played the typical "license plate" and "road sign alphabet" games. Of course, we argued over who was first to call a correct answer. As on all road trips involving my grandparents, we were promised a stop at Stuckey's for a pecan log roll. We weren't allowed to ask which exit, and my brother and I stared at each other while rolling our eyes and wagging our tongues at each exit that had the big yellow and red sign, stating "the world's best pecan candies". Since our entire family, or at least 75% of the clan, was musical, much of our trip included singing hymns, whistling, "Name that Tune", and occasionally bursting out with "Hello Muddah, Hello Fadduh" or Bobby Vinton's "It's my Party". Our grandparents would always shame us for singing that "worldly" music. At that time, my father's only job was singing and playing music on the Country Boy Eddie television show. It worked out for him to go on the trip. Mother stayed back with two small boys, and little provisions with which to get by until we returned.

Unfortunately, Daddy had already been paid and there wouldn't be another check coming until he worked again.

We made it to our 2nd cousin's house. It was a free-standing house surrounded by grass, a lake and lovely trees. It was like a movie. We had only lived in duplex housing that shared a thin wall with another family and were thrilled to see a house that also had a second story and an attic. The windows were all opened, and the front and back doors had screens that creaked when opened or shut. We introduced ourselves and I was watchful of the two older teenage girls. They were part of a Pentecostal church as well, and all the women wore skirts and/or dresses. We had dinner, sang some songs, made pallets for the children, and went to sleep. The next morning began with hot pancakes, bacon, and eggs. Their family had an organized list of chores for each member. They worked in concert washing, cleaning, taking out the garbage and so forth until everything was done. We loaded up into three cars and rode around visiting other relatives. My grandfather let two of the girl cousins ride with Michael and me in the air-conditioned car. They were used to riding in the back of a pickup truck. The next day was Sunday, and we went to Sunday School, and my brother, Michael and I sang a few specials that morning, with Daddy at the piano. Everyone enjoyed the service and we all worked up a great appetite. We came home and the women cooked a huge lunch. After lunch, most of the youth went to the front yard to play softball. We had players for two good teams, since they had invited some friends from church for lunch. Some of the men went to take a nap and the women brought chairs from the kitchen and sat under the shade to watch the game, peel some peaches for ice cream, and catch up on the family.

We were pitching the first inning, so I was way out in the field. Soon, it was our time to go to bat. I would be the last batter up. Just as the first person went up to bat, my father called out, "Janis, come here". My heart started pounding and my face certainly turned a shade of gray. 'Maybe he just wants me to go get something for him', I thought. 'I'm coming'. When I opened the screen door, he rolled his eyes and nodded toward the upstairs, and I couldn't say anything, but I shook my head "no". He gritted his teeth and clinched his fist as I hesitantly approached him while still shaking my head. He jerked me by the shoulder of my dress and started pulling and I was resistant, which enraged him. He began to drag me higher and higher, past the second floor and upward to a small, hot, dark, smelly room in the attic. He sat on a wooden box. He turned me away from him and pulled my pants down. He was forceful and sweating as he jarred me up and down from behind. I experienced a painful tare, and I felt the thick, warm substance flowing down my thighs as loud voices were shouting, "Janis.... Janis.... where are you? It's your turn to bat". As he pressed harder on both shoulders, he shoved me forward. I didn't dare look back at him as I ran out of the attic. I wiped my tears, pulled up my underwear past my sticky thighs and ran as fast as I could downstairs. By the time I reached the squeaky screen door, I had brushed on a smile and said, "I had to go to the bathroom. I'm coming".

That night, the older girls had a conversation that explained menstruation. They were telling about their friend that was pregnant and lucky, because you don't have periods when you are pregnant. They were both "on the rag", according to their own words. I picked up on it right away and acted as though I were part of the conversation. They asked if I had started yet? I naively wanted to say, "started what?", but somehow knew it would be a telling response. Later that night, I lay on the pallet thinking of the conversation with the girls, and wondered if I could get pregnant from my father. I had seen boxes of Kotex in our bathroom for years. I had been told not to ask about them. I was relieved that my situation was common to all females, so I went home and told my mother I needed my own box of Kotex now. She was floored that I knew what they were and that I was only 10 years old and already menstruating. We never had a conversation about it again, or about boys and sex. She would certainly be floored to know what had been going on for 6 years now. I sure hoped she would.

In 1985, one of the most astounding photographs of a controversial nature was taken in Columbia. A sudden eruption of the Nevado del Ruiz sent volcanic debris mixed with ice that rushed into the river and killed nearly 23,000 people. Omayra Sanchez was 13 years old and trapped beneath a slurry of mud, ice and cement for 60 hours, and died. Only her head and hands were above water. A photojournalist captured the photo, and it was later named as the World Press Photo of the Year. Her photograph is a snapshot of my life from 4-16. I was forayed upon, people were all around, even snapping photos and making home movies, but no one realized I was trapped in debris that seemed inescapable. Omayra Sanchez was forayed upon by elements of nature, and not of men. Her life ended in the exact spot where the foray occurred.

As we look again to Erikson's stages of psychosocial development, we remain at stage 4: Industry vs. Inferiority (ages 5-12). I was constantly confirming my inferiority during my 10th year. My trip to Ohio revealed the freedom and open expression shown by my distant cousins. They could even talk freely about their bodies and about boys with a giggle in their tone. My inferiority caused me to clam up in fear I would disclose something forbidden regarding my sexuality. I knew about lots of things they didn't and envied them for their innocence. All my relationships began to be held at bay. That included my mother, siblings, cousins, and even my grandparents. I dare not have a "best friend" that knew my soul secrets. Others talked about having diaries with locks on them to keep their thoughts tucked away on pages preserved for a lifetime. My thoughts were burned in my memory; every detail, smell, temperature, and word permanently written on my scarred heart.

A whole decade of life had ended, and I began to ponder the brevity of life. "Whereas ye know not what shall be on the morrow. For what is your life"? It is even a vapor, that appears for a little time, and then vanishes away" (James 4:14) Trust me, a few decades spent, I realize we all have opportunity to confront the past and reach for the future. John 10:10 says, "the thief comes to (foray: to raid and pillage) steal, kill and destroy. But, I (Jesus Christ) have come (already come and already done) that you might have life and have it more abundantly". I so identified with Omayra Sanchez when I observed her picture for the first time. My body was trapped and under the power holding me down, but my head and hands were reaching out in desperate hopes of being rescued. You have already been

MY THOUGHTS

WERE BURNED

IN MY MEMORY;

EVERY DETAIL,

SMELL,

TEMPERATURE,

AND WORD

PERMANENTLY

WRITTEN ON

MY SCARRED

HEART.

declared an overcomer but keep reading . . . . I never said you would ever be able to forget the past. We'll save our conversation about memory for another time. Do you feel in the mood for a walk? You will have to choose one of two trails. Let's get going!

"Jean Piaget - Cognitive Theory - Simply Psychology". www.simplypsychology.org.

CHAP 5
ANGEL'S TRAIL

"HAPPY TRAILS TO YOU, UNTIL WE MEET AGAIN
HAPPY TRAILS TO YOU, KEEP SMILING UNTIL THEN
WHO CARES ABOUT THE CLOUDS
   WHEN WE'RE TOGETHER?
JUST SING A SONG AND BRING THE SUNNY WEATHER.
HAPPY TRAILS TO YOU, 'TILL WE MEET AGAIN."

Happy Trails, written by Dale Evans, Recorded by Roy Rogers & Dale Evans, 1952

There was only one was to get to school every day; we walked. A couple of miles seemed endless on cold or rainy days. We were never able to afford a raincoat or an umbrella. We never owned a satchel. Most of the year, our shoes had holes in the soles. We would save cardboard and cut out a piece to fit our shoe, and it worked fine until we stepped in a puddle or walked through the rain collecting on the hot asphalt roads. To this day, I can still remember the smell of the tar as it bubbled up on the road from the intense heat. Mother would give us each a paper grocery bag to shelter us from the rain. After ascending a couple of small hills, and bending around the curves in the road, there were two paths that lay ahead. The one on the right (rightly so) we named the "angels' trail". It was a canopy of honeysuckles and wild roses in the springtime. We would often stop and pull the honeysuckle stem carefully and drink the nectar from its' blossom. The enchanting smell lingered for years as an accompaniment to my dissociating. The olfactory senses were a vibrant accessory for both the desirable and the undesirable. They carry the same power many years later.

As I am writing this chapter, we are in the early spring in Central Florida and the orange blossoms are peaking. I vividly recall the first time I smelled orange blossoms in the late 70's. My husband and I had moved to central Florida to be employed as singers in a hotel. The enchanting fragrance of orange blossoms filled the air for miles. We happened to live in an apartment that was juxtaposed to the orchard. Not long after, the oranges were harvested and taken only 4 miles away to the Orange Juice Factory. As they loaded the squeezed oranges into the massive vaults and cranked up the heat, another intoxicating aroma permeated the air for miles.

Back to school . . . The angels' trail ended with the school in sight. The devils' trail was across the road and consisted of rough and rocky terrain, kudzu vines, maypops, and all the hoodlums (pejorative hinted) that chose to smoke, drink, and cuss on their way to school. Sometimes they didn't make it to school. They played "hooky". The flashbulb memory still pops up in my thoughts of this group; the guys with their hair slicked back on the sides and swirled forward as it dangled from their foreheads, t-shirts that wanted to be white with the sleeves rolled up tight to hide cigarettes, and oh yes, one cigarette tucked behind their ear. They would have all worn black leather jackets, except they were kids from the coalmining camp, and no one owned a leather jacket. There were two girls that took the devils' trail with this lot on many occasions. One had to quit school that year, and moved away. One day, in the bathroom stall, I heard the girls talking about "S" being pregnant. I was just a kid, but I told them I was "On the rag". They laughed at me, and "S" said, "Prove it". I did, and we never really talked again. "S" came back in late summer with a baby. When school started back, she was right there on the wrong trail with different guys than the year before.

I must confess I walked the devils' trail on one occasion. I was dared by a group of girls in my class to say one curse word and I could be in the "cuss club". I knew plenty of "cuss" words and was often called many of them. That type of verbiage was commonplace in our home. I mustered up the courage to say "Damn". There! I had done it. It was the first time I had ever said such a thing. My heart was smitten, and I was certain a place was reserved for me in the fiery pits of hell. The final initiation was to walk the devils' trail. It was late in the fall and the kudzu vines were crunchy and emitted smoke when disturbed. You could smell cigarettes and liquor amid the strewn bottles and cigarette packs along the way. I froze in fear to think of the unspeakable things that could happen there. Perhaps they might be as terrible as things that happened when Daddy took me down some of the dirt trails to park the car and hide from being caught. I wondered if the pretty girl that moved away felt uncomfortable in this dirty place. I wanted to scream and cry and run at the same time, but my classmates were laughing at me to come through to the other side. Just before hyperventilating, I made it out and was told I had passed the test and was in the "cuss club" officially. It was a long night filled with regrets for me, and I knew tomorrow I would have to say a new "cuss" word to stay in the club. I couldn't bring myself to cuss again and was kicked out of the club.

I'm certain we will never know the history of the devils' trail. Some young innocent girls emerged out from that trail pregnant, raped, violated, and never the same. No doubt it was the same for some young, innocent boys as well. Those were things you overlooked back then. No one dared to engage in such conversations. No one ran home and told Mommy what happened . . . especially if what happened was at the hands of Daddy. I always remembered the cold barrel of that pistol against my head and the thoughts of my mother being dead. It was unbearable for me. What I endured was more bearable in my mind. When I came home from school the next day, my father drove me to a secluded place outside the coalmining camp. We had never been this far from home. He drove up into some bushes and I was afraid that he was going to kill me. I wondered if I deserved it because I cussed that day. Could I have a baby like the girl, "S", that went away for the summer? Is this my fault? Why does my Daddy hate me so much? My fears strengthened that he might kill me and leave me in the bushes. I had always been completely silent when we were together. He would give me directives and I obeyed. When he finished that day, I immediately started to talk about being hungry and going home, for fear he would leave me there. Everything in me wanted to curl up in my usual position with my face on the passenger window, but I had kicked into survival mode without realizing.

Erickson's fourth psychosocial stage is "Industry vs. Inferiority." During this stage, peer groups gain great significance and either fortify or lessen a child's self-esteem. For me, I was being swayed by my peers in the "cuss club", and watching the older teens use peer pressure to lure others down the devil's trail. I also realized I could make choices. I had refused to cuss the second day, and I had acquired a new skill that might save my life when my father and I were alone. I had my first encounter of feeling confident, right in line with Erickson's stage theory. However, I experienced both Industry and Inferiority simultaneously. As inferior as I may have felt during those years, another expression was breaking out to go beyond and become something more. This was empowering. Could it continue?

We all have ample opportunity to try out the devils' trail for ourselves. It was "once and done" for me. That is due to the strong ties I had with my faith. God was always watching over me, and with me, even in my darkest hours. I can honestly say I never felt God wasn't good. I often wondered whether God thought I was good enough. I didn't know why it happened, but I knew it would end someday. Proverbs 14:12 says, "There is a way (angels' trail or the devils' trail) which seemeth right unto a man, but the end thereof are the ways of death." Matthew 7:14 states, "Strait is the gate, and narrow is the way (trail), which leadeth unto life, and few there be that find it." Statistically looking at the known population of women that have been sexually abused, most resort to prostitution or to a lesbian lifestyle. My story is not even numbered in the statistics, for it was never reported. I feel for all of those still living with the secrets of past sexual abuse, and never speaking out. In the past couple of years, much talk has been in our society regarding sexual advances, harassment,

I CAN HONESTLY SAY I NEVER FELT GOD WASN'T GOOD. I OFTEN WONDERED WHETHER GOD THOUGHT I WAS GOOD ENOUGH.

and sexual favors for career and promotions among women. I have thought about them and prayed for them. My destiny is to present my story, my struggles, and all women's solutions that allow a contrite heart, a compassionate heart, and a forgiving heart to be the engine that fuels their desire for change and growth. An astounding 27.7% of women in a 1995 study were sexually abused and ended up being arrested for prostitution.

My father had a similar story to these

wayward boys frequenting the devil's trail. His family started him out on the right trail, and he decided to check out the life on the other side. He ditched more classes than he ever attended, and football was the only thing that kept him in school. He dropped out in the eleventh grade and married mother, who was in the 10th grade. Her father was a coalminer too, in another county. My dad met my mother, who was young and impressionable, at 14 years old. Mother always said she was stricken by my father's prowess on the football field and his blue eyes. His boldness seemed to run in the family. No one in the camp ever argued with "Flippo". He wasn't addressed as "Mr. Flippo" or "Curtis"; just "Flippo". He also had three brothers and two sisters. The brothers were called, "the Flippo boys". At one time, five of the six children and their families lived in the camp. Depending on the day, they could consider one another friend or foe. The community avoided confrontation with the "Flippo" boys. One time such a fight made the front page of the newspaper. Some of the brothers were drinking and began arguing, and they took the quarrel outside to protect the women and children. We ducked behind a corner coffee table and watched from the window. Two of the brothers positioned themselves behind a car and the other two were shooting from the bushes. Fortunately, no one was shot or severely injured. My dad was taken to jail and the whole family was stunned, but I was mostly thinking he wouldn't be coming in my room for at least one night.

Peer pressure and dominating personalities have taken countless people off the path that was initially intended. After repeatedly surrendering to domination and control, many yield their dreams and even their opinions to settle for much less in life. Others hold on to their values and dreams and see freedom and victory at the end. The Bible tells a story of a teenager named Joseph. He chose the angels' trail for his journey. However, he had eleven brothers trying out the devils' trail. They despised the favoritism displayed toward Joseph by their father, Jacob. (Abraham, Isaac and Jacob). They threw Joseph into a dry well in the desert, and then sold him as a slave to Israelites. He had a gift from God on his life and it caught the attention of Potiphar, captain of the guard, who had Joseph moved to the palace. Potiphar's wife desired a romantic encounter with Joseph, who quickly fled her room. Her rage at his rejection caused her to retaliate with lies that Joseph, in fact, had attacked her sexually. Joseph was cast into prison for two years and brought out to interpret a dream for the King. Joseph ultimately emerged as second only to the King. He was reunited with his family in the end. The manipulative and controlling influences of others often seemed to change Joseph's plans. He remained faithful to the path, (angels' trail) and saved an entire nation from famine and death.

You may have physically escaped the power of someone's control over your life and yet still feel the results and pain months, years, decades later. Maybe it's time to start talking and taking charge to overcome, instead of being overcome. Everything is connected to a choice. While you may feel inferior to vocalize at this juncture, you can certainly begin an internal dialogue of freedom and victory. As you submit your hidden fears, frustrations, and pain to a loving and merciful God, you will discover a load being lifted that you have carried too long. It will help guide you on the angels' trail. Every day is a new opportunity to either step into a new possibility, redo an old one that we regret, or stay trapped and stunted by the past. I am grateful God gave me the strength to press forward and keep learning. Let's head back to school . . .

(nsvrc.org/ . . . / publications_nsvrc_factsheet_media- packet_statistics-about-s . . .)
(lc.gagegroup.com/ic/ovic/ ViewpointsDetailspage/Docum entToolsPortletWindow?)

CHAP 6

SCHOOL, RULES, AND MORES

"SCHOOL DAYS, SCHOOL DAYS, DEAR
   OLD GOLDEN RULE DAYS.
READING AND 'RITING AND 'RITHMETIC
TAUGHT TO THE TUNE OF THE HICK'RY STICK"

School Days, Written in 1907 by Will D. Cobb and Gus Edwards

"School days, school days, dear old golden rule days." We sang that song the first day of school each year. Anticipation was high when the summer fades and change blows in with the cooler weather. When school resumes each year the greatest concerns of most students are whether they will impress the teacher, where they will sit in the classroom, and being able to show off their clothes, school supplies, and lunch box. School is challenging for victims of alcohol, drugs, and abuse. For us, books were barely opened in our home as children. We had no safe place to spread our books, take out a clean piece of paper, sharpen a pencil, and relax enough to focus on reading, writing, and arithmetic. There was certainly no environment to allow your creativity to unfold and process new information. We were in survival mode much of the time. As a result, the teachers completely misunderstood us as being careless and lackadaisical. The teachers were always focused on the students who were engaged and showing effort. What they didn't realize was that school could be a place for children such as myself to take a breather and not be "on guard" every second. Oftentimes, I would drift from the tasks at hand and worry about what could possibly happen when I returned home that day. I wanted desperately to be successful and to retain knowledge, but I was overwhelmed with fear and anxiety, which produces stress hormones that block our ability to process and function in a mode of learning. As a child, I always thought I wasn't smart enough.

In an article by the National Scientific Council on the Developing Child, 2010, science shows a lifelong consequence in

I WANTED DESPERATELY TO BE SUCCESSFUL AND TO RETAIN KNOWLEDGE, BUT I WAS OVERWHELMED WITH FEAR AND ANXIETY, WHICH PRODUCES STRESS HORMONES THAT BLOCK OUR ABILITY TO PROCESS AND FUNCTION IN A MODE OF LEARNING.

the developing brains of children who were exposed to persistent fear and anxiety. This "stress-system overload" dwindles a child's ability to learn and even participate in a normal social interaction throughout ones lifespan. According to numerous studies in the field of neuroscience using animal testing, results show adverse effects of elevated stress hormones such as cortisol on the brain architecture in the hippocampus and amygdala. It is beyond the scope of this book to discuss the long list of deterrents to a child's learning possibilities. Many children live with compounded lack of safety, finances, nutrition, and proper nurturing.

SAFETY: Beginning with safety, we lived with fear and anxiety most of the time. There was no structure or signal for knowing when circumstances would escalate. We each adapted our own way of coping. My teachers always shamed me for biting my nails, sucking my thumb, or twisting my hair. They were all habits associated with anxieties and fears.

FINANCES: Every family lived on a tight budget, and there may have been only a half dozen other families living near the camp that fared much better than the miners. One family owned a grocery store. Another two families were in management positions at the mines.

Some others were teacher's children that attended the school with us. There was a marked difference in the nutrition, appearance, and overall wellbeing between those students and us. They owned nice clothes, shoes, school supplies, raincoats, umbrellas, etc. When they had a toothache, they went to the dentist. When we had a toothache, our mother would put a piece of clove on the tooth, or an aspirin and tell us to bite down on it to relieve the pain. If the pain didn't go away, our Daddy would pull the tooth with a pair of pliers from his toolbox.

NUTRITION: Food in our household consisted mostly of carbohydrates. It was an affordable way to eat and feel satiated. My recollection of fresh greens and fruits are faint. I always wished we could take the vitamins called "Chocks" that was aired every Saturday morning. Two little wooden Dutch figures would come out of a cuckoo clock. They encouraged boys and girls to take their Chocks vitamins every morning. I felt a little sorry for myself when we would go to the grocery store. I would see the Chocks sitting on the shelf and dream about how they might taste, and how you could be strong and healthy. Another constant encouragement toward eating green vegetables was the cartoon character, Popeye. Families all over the nation began to buy canned spinach, after hearing reports that it contained 35 milligrams of iron in each serving. The sale of spinach increased by a third. It was later discovered that the chemist, Erich von Wolf, had misplaced a decimal point, which should have read 3.5 milligrams of iron. To provide a couple of startling examples concerning nutrition deprivation, my brother and I remember taking salt to school and salting the notebook paper and eating it in class. Salt cravings can be a sign that minerals other than sodium and chloride are missing in the diet. These can include potassium, calcium, magnesium, iron, manganese, copper, and others. Other times we would swipe our hands across dirty cars and lick our fingers. Eating earth substances such as clay or dirt is a form of pica known as geophagia. Years later a doctor friend of mine stated we could have received some benefit from the nutrients in the dirt, which contained iron and zinc. A malnourished child's behaviors can be mislabeled as mischievous, disinterested, failing to show good manners, or having a lack of focus.

RULES: As concerning rules, they were evolutionary. When a line was crossed, a punishment resulted with no forewarning. Our family didn't really talk about the topic of rules. I knew of rules in playing games such as "Tag" or "Red Rover", or even boardgames. It was straightforward.

Example: "Hide and Seek" - an old and popular children's game in which one player closes his or her eyes for a brief period (often counting to 100) while the other players hide. The seeker then opens his eyes and tries to find the hiders; the first one found is the next seeker, and the last is the winner of the round. (I'm citing the rules in case someone challenges me). For the record, we counted to 10. I never associated the word "rules" with boundaries and guidelines for families. Our Sunday school teacher taught us rules about saying, "Yes Sir, Ma'am, and Thank You." I must say, I didn't accept everything she taught as "truth", because she once told us that grownups are always right, we should never talk back to them, and always obey them. The bizarre thing about that teacher is she always ordered her husband around, and it worked. He was a good student, I suppose. In our family, the biggest rule we learned was that we didn't talk to anyone about things that happened in our home. Mother was as protective as Daddy of that rule. She didn't want to be perceived as weak and vulnerable. I recall a commercial years ago about Las Vegas that ended with the phrase, "What happens in Vegas, stays in Vegas". That also seemed to be the guidelines in our family. The convincing part about never telling others what happened in our home was that no one would like me or ever invite our family over if we talked about our problems. My lips were sealed.

In her book, Toxic Parents, Overcoming Their Hurtful Legacy and Reclaiming Your Life, Dr. Susan Forward states the seven most common types of toxic parents. They are:

1) The godlike parents, where the child's independence is suffocated. Children of these types of parents are given a message that they cannot survive without the parent. "Look what I do for you."

2) The inadequate parents, where the child becomes almost invisible. Parents place their focus on their own survival, instead of nurturing the child's needs.

3) The controllers, where the child is only an extension of the family. "You just listen to us and don't ask questions when we tell you what we are doing", (where we are going, what we are eating, etc.)

4) The verbal abusers, who directly or indirectly humiliate a child over and over. The abuse can be direct or indirect. The direct approach would say, "You're dumber than a door." The indirect approach would use sarcasm, teasing, and cynicism.

5) Competitive parents, where the child is always compared to a smarter, prettier, stronger child. "Why can't you be like so and so?"

6) The physical abusers, where there is no place to hide, no escape from physical punishment from the active abuser.
7) The passive abuser – these stand by as the active abuser acts out their abuse. The passive abuser is essentially abandoning the child. Oftentimes, these are the enablers to the active abusers, as they take no action.
8) The alcoholics, where all the behaviors above are present.
9) The sexual abusers, which represents the ultimate betrayal.

I could certainly relate to numbers 2-9 on the list. They all seemed to amalgamate into one motus of operandi. This book only confirmed what I had come to know as an adult about my upbringing.

I have accumulated a few rules of my own regarding healthy parenting over the years. I certainly did not implement them all from the beginning, but over time, I noted my own "Ten Commandments for Parenting" that I feel are worthy of passing to my posterity. They are:

1) Verbalize your thoughts and feelings for your children. Don't assume they know you love them by

what you do. They need to hear your voice, feel your affection, and see the love in your expression.

2) Allow their opinion to be heard, without cutting them off and telling them they are wrong. You will learn much more about where your child is in the developmental stage by hearing their thoughts. It's not to say they are right, or that you will not correct in the end. However, it will carry much greater weight when they feel validated.

3) Never ask, "What's wrong with you, anyway?" Children interpret this literally and feel not only that something is wrong with them, but that they are, in fact, wrong.

4) Never say, "You don't love me like you used to." Many parents have used transference from other relationships and put it on their children. The maturation of a child brings changes and shifts in their hormones and chemical cocktail. While the visible "signs" of a child's love might not be as obvious as once expressed, it is revealed in different ways throughout development.

5) Never seek to establish shame and guilt when the child makes a mistake or misbehaves. Demonstrate the unconditional love you would desire.

6) Establish the rules in advance, and not once the offense had occurred. Proverbs 22:6 instructs parents to "Train up a child in the way he should go". This indicates establishing the guidelines in advance, along the way, and with consideration to the age of the child. These will vary over time. The principle, however, will remain the same. Each family must develop their own set of core values.
7) Set up consequences that are in direct relation to the behavior, or event. It is wise to instruct in advance, rather than react after the fact. "Grounded for life" is a preposterous response for any behavior.
8) Check your heart, to insure you are not acting out of pain and hurt from you own childhood. Avoid comments such as, "You don't know what it was like to go to bed hungry. Now, eat everything on that plate."
9) Be vulnerable when stepping into new territory as your child matures. A wise parent will adjust along with the maturing child. These seasons of change bring a level of maturity to both child and parent.
10) Don't allow your child to believe you have all the answers. You will end up destroying them by allowing them to think you can solve their life issues.

This could lead to co-dependency, which can be passed from generation to generation.

MANNERS: Any manners I acquired as a young child are to be credited to observation in public places or, MGM, Looney Tunes, Lassie, and Captain Kangaroo. It was not until adulthood that I realized the old black and white movies, the cartoons, and television programs were more than random forms of entertainment. They all generally had a character that focused on a specific subject, perhaps failed somewhere in the middle, and then corrected mistakes and learned from them. I could always identify with Shirley Temple movies. She always played the role of the deprived child with greater struggles than most, but ultimately rose in victory with someone to love her. She seemed to show the negative effects of being ill-mannered, and the reward for exhibiting good manners. I gathered manners by observation as a child. Today there are many resources available. Sheryl Eberly, author of "365 Manners Kids Should Know', emphasizes 10 key manners parents should teach their children. They are:

1) Stand to show respect

2) Be aware of others' physical space in public

3) Show respect for your elders

4) Acknowledge others entering and exiting your home, including Mom and Dad.
5) Learn and remember people's names.
6) Kids shouldn't be the center of attention all the time.
7) Change the subject politely.
8) Don't point or stare at people
9) Be considerate and kind to people with disabilities.
10) Be a good guest.

DEATH: As death is not a subject often discussed in most families, it should at least be addressed to prepare the child for the inevitable. Parents are best suited for answering the difficult questions children ponder concerning death. A caveat: if you are considering the discussion with your child; get your theology and philosophy in order before you present something you can't undo. Some parents use metaphors to explain death that create more fears and questions in the life of the child. Example: A young girl died when I was small, and an adult told me that "God needed a flower for His garden, and He picked her." I have heard that metaphor many times since, and it is a frightful vision of God. I could imagine Him possibly wanting to pick me every night when it was time for bed. John 10:10 declares, "the thief (enemy) cometh not, but for to steal, and to kill, and to destroy: I am come that they might have life, and that they might have it more abundantly." From the sin of Adam and Eve, we now live in a fallen world. Everything is in a process of fading and dying. Viruses, diseases, maladies, disabilities and aging bring decay and ultimately, death. When we understand the completion of a meaningful life, we can have hope for eternity.

Regarding death, much came too early for me. My grandparents were pastors of Pentecostal churches for nearly 50 years. When a death occurred in the coal-mining camp, the deceased was placed on the dining room table in the center of the living room and relatives and friends would bring food and congregate into the night for two to four days. My brother, Michael, and I began singing at these "wakes" before I started school. No one ever instructed or taught us the etiquette surrounding loss and death. We had adopted our own defense mechanisms for coping with the chaos and stress in our home by using humor, which didn't work well in death settings. On these plenteous occasions, we would scurry about the rooms of the house, nibbling from the buffet of foods, giggling at any opportunity and even at times approaching the dead body and touching it. We mostly went undetected, but I recall more than once getting a good smack from my grandparents. To my regret, no one offered instruction, but somehow left you feeling you were a big disappointment and an embarrassment to the family for not figuring out these concepts for yourself. That was, indeed, an underlying theme in general. Everything will make the FAMILY look bad. The truth was the family was suffering on so many levels.

III. MORES
(developing child.NET Persistent Fear and Anxiety
Can Affect Young Children's Learning and
*Nutricioncare.net JUDY CONVERSE MPH RD LDN Development) *brainpickings.org The True Science of Spinach and What the Popeye Mythology Teaches Us About How Error Spreads/Maria Popova
(Livestrong.com Licking and vitamin deficiencies in children, Krista Sheehan. ref 2, page 183) (ref 8, last paragraph page 407)
https://www.britannica.com/topic/hide-and- seek-game
*Parenting.com/10 Manners Parents Should be Teaching Their Kids But Aren't, Ellen Sturm Niz/365 Manners Kids Should Know

CHAP 7
FROZEN

"THE SNOW BLOWS WHITE ON THE MOUNTAIN TONIGHT
NOT A FOOTPRINT TO BE SEEN
A KINGDOM OF ISOLATION, AND IT
   LOOKS LIKE I'M THE QUEEN
THE WIND IS HOWLING LIKE THE SWIRLING STORM INSIDE
COULDN'T KEEP IT IN, HEAVEN KNOWS I TRIED...
DON'T LET THEM IN, DON'T LET THEM SEE
BE THE GOOD GIRL, YOU ALWAYS HAVE TO BE
CONCEAL, DON'T FEEL, DON'T LET THEM KNOW...".

Let It Go, Songwriters: Kristen Anderson-Lopez & Robert
Lopez. Copyright Walt Disney Music Company

In the summer of 1964, I was soon to be 12. I was elated to be in an outdoor play for the last day of school and the May Pole Dance. I was in a small skit and wore a tattered robe representing Cinderella. At the director's que, I dropped the filthy robe and revealed a blue chiffon dress (borrowed from my classmate, whose father owned a grocery store). Lyndon Johnson was president that year, after the assassination of JFK earlier in November of 1963. I didn't realize my walk home on the angel's trail would be my last one ever. The trail still carried the fragrance of honeysuckles and roses. It was a bittersweet day. When we came home from school, we were told we would be moving up north to Indiana. The coalmining industry was dwindling, and many were being laid off work. There were rumors of many available jobs in Gary, Indiana at the Bethlehem Steel Mill. Daddy had two uncles, one aunt, and several cousins living there, and he decided we would relocate that summer. Michael and I were devastated, but unable to voice our thoughts or feelings. The unspoken rule was to go along with whatever Daddy wanted. That went for mother as well as us children. We had all suffered the consequences of alternative opinions.

As Michael and I had grown accustomed to traveling on the weekends from church to church in the Southeast, we couldn't comprehend that life as we knew it would come to a drastic freeze. These weekend events included not only our denomination, but many other churches that engaged in weekend singings and "dinner on the ground", as it was called back then. These events represented the social life of churchgoers. There would be Sunday morning service, piano and guitars for the musicians, while the women prepared the food. Everyone enjoyed a great meal together, and then went back to church for an afternoon singing, which lasted 2-3 hours. There was at least one guest group or singer present that was the feature talent. We met a great friend during those years whose name was Ronnie Horton. Ronnie was blind from birth. However, he compensated with phenomenal abilities to recite the scriptures, sing, and play the piano. We travelled in the same circuits of churches, and always looked forward to being with Ronnie. Church is where my brother Michael and I spent most weekends. Both sets of grandparents, all uncles, aunts, and cousins lived within 15 miles of one another. Most of them could sing or play an instrument. Church was a life source for us. We did not take the idea of moving casually. I wasn't good at making new friends for fear they might ask me something personal or cause me to blurt out something I would regret. Before we had too much time to bemoan the move, we were loaded up and on the road.

I slept most of the trip to Indiana. My Father was driving the truck with all our belongings, and only a space for the driver. My mother followed behind in the car that was packed to the max with four children and anything else we could cram in between. Years later, I would see a movie that reminded me of our family the year we moved up north. It is a phenomenal movie about a dysfunctional family from 1979 titled, "The Great Santini". Robert Duvall plays a narcissistic, drunken, menace to his wife, and four children. There are so many similarities between the movie and my upbringing. Just as in the movie, my oldest brother was constantly having to prove his manhood to Daddy. If Daddy felt Michael didn't "man up" in situations, then he took matters into his own hands. It would often lead to openly shaming Michael, forcing him to stand up for himself, and once Daddy even went to our high school and punched Michael's coach out. He somehow saw all of us as poor extensions of himself.

When he was in that type of mindset, we all ended up taking hits and strikes. We always felt it was our fault because he would tell us that exact thing. The Great Santini (Robert Duvall) demonstrated much of the dysfunctional features we witnessed everyday growing up. I was entering middle school, and Michael was in the ninth grade. We both endured bullying regularly in one form or another. Our clothes weren't very nice. We couldn't afford to buy the lunch and so we made banana sandwiches every day. The students laughed at me and said, "the hillbilly is eating monkey burgers". My self-esteem was already poor, and it seemed this new set of circumstances was taking it to a new level.

Fortunately, we located a church of the same denomination we grew up attending. Sunday came with both anticipation and hesitation. Our parents didn't attend church and it was up to us to find transporation. The pastor contacted one of the members living close by, and Sunday morning a small car slowly pulled up to the curb of the house. An older woman was clinching the steering wheel and leaning forward. She slowly rolled down the window and with a big smile said, "Is Michael and Janis here?" She was adorable. When we got in the back seat, she gave us both a once over as she tilted her head back to see through the glasses resting low on her nose. The moment we got in the car, she introduced herself as "Sister Evelyn Harris", and suggested we all begin to pray out loud in concert, because her gas tank was registering empty. Her husband didn't attend church, and she said we would have to exercise our faith to get there and back. We made it there and went inside, where we were greeted with so much acceptance and love. Immediately, the pastor asked us to stand up and introduce ourselves, and to sing a special song. I felt at home and apologized to God for resisting the move. I knew then He was leading and directing my life. It was still a trial to trust anyone, even God. When service concluded, we got back in Sister Harris' car and prayed all the way home, with the gas indicator pointing to empty. Evelyn Harris would prove to be an instructor for building faith in my and Michael's life.

Soon, Michael and I became a vital part of the youth group, music department, and Bible Quiz team. Church, once again, was our social life. However, school was challenging. I had come from a school of about 100 to a school with 3000 students. Because of my interest in music, I joined the school choir and glee club. My ear for music helped my lack of ability in reading the notes. I was also taking Spanish 101 that semester, my introduction to languages. By mid-September we were settling into our house. This was the first time we ever lived in a home that had locks on the interior doors. I remember my mother was in the bathroom with the door locked, and my Daddy kicked the door down and broke all the locks in every room and told us we weren't having locks, ever! Well, alrighty then! The weather turned chilly early up North, and I recall many frigid nights on my side with my knees drawn, and my hands tucked between my legs. With my nightly prayer, I begged God to please keep my Daddy away. But, when I felt his hands, I lay perfectly still, as though I were dead. He would move me around, and position my body, and I was in a state of tonic immobility. However, at the time, I didn't know why I responded in such a way. It is worth mentioning the defense behaviors that are automatic within each of us. People who are victims of sexual abuse may experience several, all, or skip directly to tonic immobility.

Imagine a scenario in which a young teenage girl is approached by a young man that is about her size. Suppose he reaches out to snatch her from the street and into the alley. The series of automatically activated defense behaviors, also known as the "defense cascade" are as follows:

1) Arousal (alerting danger). This is popularly known as the beginning stages of the flight or fight stage.

2) Freezing. This is a momentary time for the brain to assess the situation. During these seconds, motor programs in the brain to assist in escaping or resisting involve releasing high- energy and non-opioid analgesia (painkiller) to empower the victim to run or fight.

3) Fight or Flight. The victim has every intention to fight, kick, scream, and escape. However, suppose the attacker puts a knife to her throat.

4) Tonic Immobility - Immediately, the brain switches patterns and immobility programs are activated, which cause a type of paralysis. Now, the arousal system shuts off and there is a release of "opioid analgesia" to reduce fear and pain. The victim knows there is no way of escape, and the body is paralyzed temporarily.

5) Collapsed Immobility (fainting in fear). When the attack continues, the opioid is released even greater, and fainting from fear is the next in this cascade defense. Victims have no control over these series of behaviors. They initiate from sensory inputs of touch, smell, sight, feel, and taste that peak when no escape is possible.

6) Quiescent Immobility. This involves the body's ability to release a state of rest that promotes healing and restoring. Victims of sexual abuse, rape, as well as PTSD military veterans have experienced the cascade of defenses at varying degrees. Victims that experienced tonic immobility were twice as likely to suffer PTSD, and three times more likely to suffer severe depression following the attack.

This is a tool that may be helpful in rape cases, and even sexual abuse cases when they are drilled about the events and even asked, "Did you fight back?" "Did you scream out?" The guilt and shame of the event is relived all over again with such questions. They may even ask themselves, "Is it my fault? Why did I not fight back? "In some jurisdictions, resistance is necessary for a legal definition of rape. Understanding this cascading defense mechanism can be liberating for many who have been unaware of the idea of tonic immobility.

There is also something worth including known as "Learned Helplessness". Learned helplessness, according to Martin Seligman, is a phenomenon observed in both humans and other animals when they have been conditioned to expect pain, suffering, or discomfort without a way to escape it. Eventually, after enough conditioning, the animal will stop trying to avoid the pain at all-even if there is an opportunity to truly escape it. It is called "learned" helplessness because no one is born with the belief that they have no control whatsoever regarding what happens to them. It is learned over time and circumstances.

We were beginning to feel a sense of community with our new friends and church life. The weather turned freezing cold early in the fall, and snow began to flurry during a Sunday night service. We had to brush the snow from Sister Harris' windshield and skidded a few times on the slippery roads on the way home. It was our first experience with snow. We had no coats, gloves, earmuffs, or scarves. I recall Daddy taking our family to a department store that Friday afternoon and having each of us pick out coats, and all accessories needed for the cold weather. He ripped the tags off and made us walk out the door. My parents had an argument about the experience, and Daddy drove us all home and we didn't see him until the wee hours of Sunday morning. He had knocked on the door multiple time in a drunken stupor, but Mother wouldn't let him in. I could hear him crying outside my window. I felt so bad for him as I peeked through the foggy windowpane, but didn't dare interfere with what happened between him and Mother. He slept in the front yard with a snow-covered ground for his bed. Just a few nights earlier, I lay in a frozen state as he disturbed my sleep; now he was the one freezing in the snow . . . but my sleep was still disturbed.

By Erikson's psychosocial stage theory, I was in the Identity vs. Isolation stage (ages 12-18), which should result in the virtue of love. This stage should be the time adolescents experience and express interest in possible boyfriends or girlfriends. Infatuations are heightened during this phase, for those who transition in a proper environment. I recall watching "I Dream of Jeannie" and "Bewitched" during those years. They were magical, and not authentic women, and I didn't seem to consider my thoughts of love or being loved. For me, life was mostly inside my head. When it was time to laugh, sing, work, or whatever, I robotically engaged for the sake of the moment. I can only explain by saying I didn't have room in my head to dissociate and daydream at the same time. When I felt pushed to the limits, I leaned on dissociating to lessen the pressure. Therefore, daydreaming had no place in life during these years. This broken girl needed help desperately. My feelings were iced over, and I couldn't imagine what could possibly thaw my frozen soul. I wasn't

IT IS IMPORTANT TO REALIZE WE ARE A TRIPARTITE BEING, AND GOD CREATED US TO CONNECT TO HIM SPIRITUALLY, AND FOR OUR SOUL TO RESPOND TO OUR SPIRIT, AND FOR OUR PHYSICAL BEING TO BEHAVE ACCORDINGLY.

mature enough to understand that God wanted me to be fulfilled in my Spirit, Soul, and Body. I was compartmentalized in that regard. It is important to realize we are a tripartite being, and God created us to connect to Him spiritually, and for our soul to respond to our spirit, and for our physical being to behave accordingly. There is a God-ordained flow that brings fulfillment through every part of our life. When we, for instance, allow our thoughts to exalt themselves above

God (2 Corinthians 10:5) we will despair. The Bible instructs us to reject the thoughts that do not line up with the Word of God. King David was at a crossroads in his life when he had committed adultery with another man's wife, had him murdered on the frontlines of the battlefield, and lost the newborn son of the adulterous affair. He cried out to God and said: "Search me, O God, and know my heart: try me, and know my thoughts: And see if there be any wicked way in me and lead me in the way everlasting." (Psalm 139:23, 24). "Let the words of my mouth, and the meditation of my heart, be acceptable in thy sight, O Lord, my strength, and my redeemer. (Psalm 19:14) David is referring to his spirit, soul, and body in this urgent prayer. He realized he had failed in his moral behavior and was asking God to search both his spirit and his thoughts (soul) for renewal and forgiveness.

It is essential to know God wants to communicate with us on all three levels. He obviously cares that our spirit is reborn, so that we will spend eternity with Him. He also tells us we can pray for the blessings of heaven to come to earth in our thoughts and bodies. The idea of renewing the mind is only possible through Jesus Christ, the Son of God. The apostle Paul puts it this way in Ephesians 4:21-24: "If so be that you have heard him (Jesus Christ), and have been taught by him, as the truth is in Jesus: That you put off concerning the former conversation the old man, which is corrupt according to the deceitful lusts; And be renewed in the spirit of your mind; And that you put on the new man, which after God is created in righteousness and true holiness." The "old man" refers to the way you used to think and process. Once you are made new by accepting Jesus, it is as if you take off the old person you were and put on a new person. When Paul mentioned being renewed in the spirit of your mind, the Greek meaning is to get a new mental disposition about life, both now and for eternity. You will still live in the same world, but you will approach it with confidence and hope, instead of inferiority and despair.

The warmth of knowing Jesus melts away all that is frozen and rigid in your thinking. You have a new outlook in the life God wants you to live.

King David came to the end of himself and repented for all his sins and failures with the famous prayer of Psalm 51:

1) Have mercy upon me, O God, according to thy lovingkindness: according unto the multitude of thy tender mercies blot out my transgressions.

2) Wash me thoroughly from mine iniquity and cleanse me from my sin.

3) For I acknowledge my transgressions: and my sin is ever before me.
4) Against thee, thee only, have I sinned, and done this evil in thy sight: that thou mightest be justified when thou speakest, and be clear when thou judgest.
5) Behold, I was shapen in iniquity; and in sin did my mother conceive me.
6) Behold, thou desirest truth in the inward parts: and in the hidden part thou shalt make me to know wisdom.
7) Purge me with hyssop, and I shall be clean: wash me, and I shall be whiter than snow.
8) Make me to hear joy and gladness; that the bones which thou hast broken may rejoice.
9) Hide thy face from my sins and blot out all mine iniquities.
10) Create in me a clean heart, O God; and renew a right spirit within me.
11) Cast me not away from thy presence; and take not thy holy spirit from me.
12) Restore unto me the joy of thy salvation; and uphold me with thy free spirit.

King David got up from that prayer and took back the crown as King and conquered his enemies. However, his sins came with a great price. He suffered loss in his relationships with his children and lived with much regret. That is an Old Testament event. Today, because of Jesus, we can live with a new attitude, knowing our sins have been covered by the death of Jesus on the Cross.

Article: "Fear and the Defense Cascade: Clinical Implications and Management" (doi: 10.1097/HRP.0000000000000065) 1970 (Abramson, L.Y., Seligman, M.E.P. & Teasdale, J.D. (1978).
Learned helplessness in humans: Critique and reformulation.
JournalofAbnormalPsychology, 87,49- Doi:10.1037/0021-843X.87.1.49).

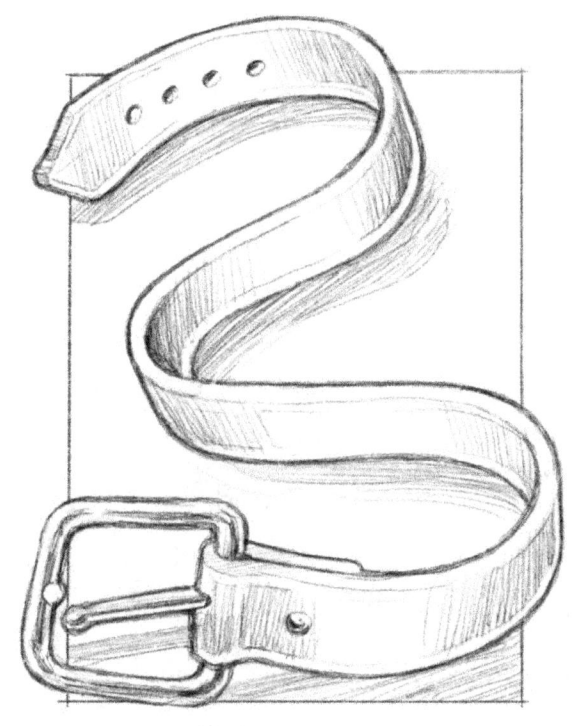

CHAP 8
THE WHIPPING

"BE A GOOD GIRL, YOU'VE GOTTA'
   TRY A LITTLE HARDER
THAT SIMPLY WASN'T GOOD
   ENOUGH TO MAKE US PROUD
... HOW MANY TIMES DO I
   HAVE TO TELL YOU?
... THE LEAST YOU CAN
   DO IS KEEP QUIET"

Perfect, song by Alanis Morissette, 1995, Songwriters: Alanis Nadine Morissette & Glen Ballard. Copyright Concord Music Publlishing LLC, Universal Music Publishing Company

Report cards were always a tense time for us children. Due to the dysfunctionality and lack of support at home, we all struggled with school. We geared up for a whipping on report card day. I lallygagged as long as possible to prolong the inevitable during the first grading period of seventh grade. The adjustments from the south to north, from elementary school with one teacher to maintaining a locker, changing classes from one floor to another was enough, without giving thought to my home life. As we stated earlier, neuroscientists have discovered changes in the hippocampus and prefrontal cortex in children of trauma and sexual abuse. It can even be permanent in some cases.

Our brother, Steve, came home from school that day with a report card and a letter. The letter informed my parents that Steve was placed in a class for children with learning disabilities. His teacher proceeded to say he was not at the rate of learning with his classmates and should be kept in a special class. My father was mixing drugs and alcohol during these years, and when my mother showed him the report card and letter, he summoned Steve to the living room. All of us were afraid of Daddy, but Steve was harmless and unable to even describe his feelings appropriately. To begin with, Steve was only 7, and the letter was written in cursive. Daddy put Steve on his lap, opened the letter, and said, "Read this to me, boy." Steve looked terrified and said, "Daddy, I-I-I can't read." He always stuttered when he was nervous or caught off guard. Daddy said, "What do you mean you can't read? What's the matter with you?" He slapped him across the face with the back of his hand. Up until now, I was crouched behind the door at the end of the hallway listening. I peeked around and saw him slap him again and say, "Read it, you little chicken shit." Steve was crying so pitifully and shaking his head in disappointment as he repeated, "I-I-I can't read, I can't read." I emerged from the hallway and looked at Daddy with disdain, as my arms were stiffened close by my side with clinched fists, and I tried to be bold and said, "If you want to hit on somebody, why don't you hit on me?" He knocked Steve out of the chair and lunged toward me and pushed me into the bedroom. I felt a surge of adrenaline and momentarily prepared to stand straight and take whatever came at me. The first whip of the belt slammed my body onto the bed, and I clinched my fists and closed my eyes for the duration. Mother was begging him to stop. Steve was crying and Daddy was

THE FIRST WHIP OF THE BELT SLAMMED MY BODY ONTO THE BED, AND I CLINCHED MY FISTS AND CLOSED MY EYES FOR THE DURATION.

beating me with a thick leather belt. He was so mad that he was hitting me with the buckle too. "Have you had enough?" he mocked. I wanted to get up and say something in retaliation, but I just couldn't get up. I doubted Steve's fragile body could have taken the hits without some sort of internal injury. I couldn't go to school for 3 days. When I finally went, I had to wear black tights so no one could see my legs, and I had to change in the bathroom stall for gym class so no one would see my back. Mother never offered a word of comfort in private or mentioned it again. She did say, however, that I should watch how I talk to my dad.

In hindsight, there is not one single memory of Daddy whipping, spanking, or whatever reference one would make to the behavior, that was out of desire and concern to teach us a value or life lesson. His face always reflected anger and disgust, and never the "This hurts me more than it hurts you" approach we often hear in fictions and in the movies. There were several occasions where no one took the responsibility for the "crime" that was committed, and we all had to take a whipping. However, my baby brother never had a hand laid upon him to my knowledge. There was no reasoning to the whippings. If we didn't wash the car to his standards, we were whipped. If we didn't shine his shoes for his nighttime "honky tonk" work properly, we were whipped. No one dared to take the time to show us how to meet the standard, but unknown consequences were implemented with no prior explanation.

My dad had lots of whippings as a boy. I've heard stories of broomsticks, electrical cords, tree switches, and other items used for the whipping. One incident stands out above the rest concerning his childhood. He once told us children that as a pubescent young boy, his mother had a girlfriend over for a visit. When my dad came in the kitchen door, she gave an overview of the wrong he had committed and ordered him to strip down right in front of her girlfriend. She proceeded to whip him. That's all I know of the story, but enough to realize the shame and humiliation he must have suffered, even regarding his sexuality, that possibly troubled him for his lifetime.

Once, Daddy came home around 2 or 3 in the morning and demanded, as always, that we all wake up and come to the living room. Mother was tired from cleaning all day and made a comment to that effect. The next thing Michael and I knew, Daddy took hold of Mother with one hand and began punching and slapping with the other. Michael and I tried to jump on him and stop the violence. He took his shoe off and began hitting Michael with it. I tried kicking and stepping on his feet, but he was as a wild animal when the adrenaline and effects of drugs and alcohol were empowering him. He seemed invincible at that moment, and within less than five minutes, he was sitting on the couch sound asleep. The breakfast Mother cooked sat in the kitchen uneaten, and we silently went to our rooms to bed, Mother with a bloody mouth. We never had conversation among ourselves concerning the events that had occurred. I have one small story of stepping up and taking a beating for someone else. For those reading along for my journey, perhaps you stood in another's place that should have suffered the guilt and blame.

God looked down upon the beautiful earth He created and saw it was filled with evil. In the book of Genesis God instructed Noah to build an ark of safety to house pairs of animals, plants, and humans as progenitors of the future world. However, this purge failed at providing atonement for the sins of mankind. The world was divided between those who struggled and failed at keeping the commandments, and those who blatantly served and worshipped false gods. Prophecies foretold of a Savior that would become the ultimate sacrifice for all the sins of the world. His name would be Jesus, the Son of God. The prophecy was the only ray of hope until an angel appeared to a virgin named Mary (Luke 1:26-38) confirming that she (Mary) would be the vessel used of God to deliver this Messiah, born of the Holy Spirit. The story is the most beautiful one ever told! The baby was born, angels, shepherds and kings came to worship Him. This Savior was indeed the hope for all mankind.

However, He emerged at the age of 30 and became a great controversy among the political leaders, as well as the Jewish Rabbis of the day. His quotes of being God brought great offense to the religious sects. The idea of being the King of Kings certainly threatened the empires of the regions.

But Jesus Christ, the Son of God, left the grandeur of heaven, crossed the portal of eternity into the earthly realm and willingly became the sacrificial Lamb offered once for all. The Political and religious leaders joined forces in making false accusations in an all-out effort to rid themselves of One who welcomed all races, genders, socio-economic statuses, educational standings, and no prior religious affiliations. They were abhorred by His declaration of being the Great I Am and a proponent of a new commandment of Love. Strongly influenced by demonic forces, this band of both religious and political leaders crucified the Savior on a cross. He was beaten beyond recognition, and His hands and feet were nailed to a cross. Just before His last breath, He cried, "Father, forgive them". When He spoke the final words, "It is finished," He bowed His head and died. The earth quaked and the skies grew dark. He was buried in a borrowed tomb that was sealed shut with a large stone covering the entrance. On the third day, the stone was rolled away and the tomb was vacant. Jesus Christ, the Messiah, had accomplished His mission.

He appeared to some 500 people over the next few weeks and returned to the Father in Heaven.

Have you ever brought this story into your personal life? Could you imagine this same Jesus seeing you in His heart thousands of years ago? He saw you before you were born. He knew you would be right where you are at this moment. He spoke to a group in Matthew 11:28-29 (KJV) v.28, "Come unto me, all ye that labour and are heavy laden, and I will give you rest. Take my yoke upon you and learn of me; for I am meek and lowly in heart: and ye shall find rest unto your souls."

His offer still stands. Are you exhausted trying to live life with all the hurts and difficulties alone? Perhaps you have tried to bury them in your own tomb with a stone-cold heart covering. I cautiously protected my pain and suffering, convinced that no one could possibly understand my convoluted Pandora's box. We were designed from the beginning to connect back to God, finding a lasting relationship that will not only bring fulfillment and hope, but also bear our burdens, understand us in our weaknesses and strengths, and accept us as we truly are. Consider making a change that will result in an assurance of eternal life. If you're changing, you're not the only one. More changes are ahead . . .

CHAP 9
CHANGES

... EVERYBODY'S CHANGING AND I DON'T KNOW WHY
SO LITTLE TIME
TRY TO UNDERSTAND THAT I'M
TRYING TO MAKE A MOVE JUST TO STAY IN THE GAME
I TRY TO STAY AWAKE AND REMEMBER MY NAME
BUT EVERYBODY'S CHANGING AND
   I DON'T FEEL THE SAME

Everybody's Changing, Recorded by Keane, 2003, Songwriters: Tim Rice-Oxley, Tom Chaplin, Richard Hughes. Copyright Universal Music Publishing Mgb. Ltd.

Life had become rather predictable in 1966. Michael and I were permanent fixtures in our little church. Sister Harris still picked us up every Sunday and Wednesday. My best friend was Cheryl Johnson. We became friends when I was still 11 and we first moved to Indiana. Our grandparents knew each other back in the south, and it gave us an instant connection. I knew we would be best friends for life; and I was right! I spent the night with her about once a month, but I never wanted her to stay over with me. Her home was beautiful, and I felt so safe when I was there. When it came to our family, we could expect some nice days with family and friends, and sometimes a week with no fighting and yelling.

Steve was settled into special classes and progressing well. He was a great brother to us, and especially to our baby brother Dirk. Dirk and Steve could always be found outside digging up dirt, playing cops and robbers, and building forts and castles from sheets and tarp. Dirk was undoubtedly the pick of the litter, and we didn't resent him for it. After all, he was the baby and the last child. It wasn't any fault of his that he got superior treatment.

In the summer of '67, I got my first job at Dunkin' Donuts on Indianapolis Blvd. in Hammond, Indiana. It was between two and three miles from home, and only one mile from school. It was a great distraction. I was ready for something in life I could offer that would bring satisfaction. It's remarkable how much joy a frosted donut with sprinkles and a hot cup of coffee can be for a customer running in from the freezing snow. I quickly learned how to glaze the fresh donuts, frost them, fill them, and I especially enjoyed eating them! Every Saturday I could take home a few dozen of the ones that didn't sell the day before. I had a sense of contributing to the family for the first time. Michael worked across the street at a McDonald's, and he also brought home bags of free McDonald's on Saturdays. Without question, Saturday became everyone's favorite.

My Dad continued to play music at the club and the style of his band was shifting from merely country to a blend of country with rock 'n roll. He had maintained enough income to become part owner of the club. It became more than a weekend music gig, and more of a business. "Hanky Panky" by Tommy James and the Shondells was in the top billboard hits that year and was the style of music my Daddy played well. His wardrobe during those years were Nehru shirts. Those were the shirts with short, Mandarin collars that stood up, and had many buttons all the way down. The shirt tails were longer and straight across. It was a nod to the Beatles. The Beatles had turned to Eastern Religion and fashioned their clothes after Jawaharlal Nehru, the first Prime Minister of India.

Mother went through some significant changes that year herself. She had battled problems with her teeth and had them pulled and got brand new dentures. When her teeth were initially pulled, they put stitches in, and she had to wait two weeks for her gums to heal and for the dentures to arrive. She had a fever the first few days, and I was frightened at the thought of something happening to her. I knew Daddy would be coming into my room, because I had figured out by now that he approached me when something was awry between the two of them. I remember them getting into a fight because he called her an "old bag". She said, "Curtis, don't say that". He slapped her that day, and she had to go back and get stitches repaired in her mouth. It was a long two weeks to be seen with no teeth for a young woman in her early thirties. He mocked and laughed at her many times during and after the incident with her teeth. She started wearing makeup and dying her hair. On the weekends, she would even go out to the club with Daddy and have a few drinks.

Michael and I decided we were going to kill our Daddy the next time he hit mother. We would both take a heavy iron skillet and hit him in the head when he was beating mother. That was our plan. I don't even know what that next fight was about, but I just remember Daddy unscrewing the leg off the piano stool and taking it and striking Mother. He was blocking the door to the kitchen, and we were trying to push him away, but instead he knocked us down and kept on hitting Mother. Michael stood back up and Daddy hit him in the mouth. Mother screamed for us to get the boys and run outside. We grabbed them from their beds as Mother ran out the door. Daddy just stayed in the house and slammed the door shut. Mother was bleeding from her eye and mouth as we ran from neighbor to neighbor. They all said they would call the police, but they couldn't get involved because they were afraid of what Daddy would do to them. Mother begged them not to get the police involved. We weren't dressed properly, had no shoes on, and it was in the middle of the night. Mother knocked on a stranger's door down the street, and they let her use the phone to call my Daddy's uncle across town. He picked us up an hour later and we hid out for three days at their house. They finally told Daddy where we were, and he came and picked us up. I understood it was a lot to take care of a woman and four children in despair.

The big change for the 1967-68 year was that Michael was a high school senior, and he would be moving to Alabama when he graduated. He planned to live with my aunt and uncle, go to college, and play the piano for their trio every weekend. His move would bring change for me. Michael and I were inseparable from the near drowning incident when we were toddlers. We were seldom seen apart. Even though he didn't know of our family "secret", I couldn't imagine his absence when I was feeling desperate and needed uplifting. We always managed to laugh no matter what we were facing. I wondered if I could laugh alone. His graduation was so exciting, because he was the first one in our entire family to graduate from High School. The next week, Michael and I left, as usual, to spend the summer in Alabama. The difference was, he would be staying when summer ended. I stayed with my grandparents, and Michael moved his things in with my aunt and Uncle. We attended summer camp, youth gatherings, state conventions and ended the summer at the General Assembly in Cleveland, Tennessee. It was the headquarters for the denomination to which we had belonged our whole lives.

When school resumed, I was able to get my job back at Dunkin' Donuts. I felt a sense of loss with Michael gone and showed many signs of depression. During the early weeks of school, I started eating to console my emotional hunger. I could feel myself gaining weight every day. Eating was something to do when I felt depressed, and it seemed to help while I was eating or snacking. Oddly enough, my Daddy had lost 40-50 pounds when we were in Alabama that summer. During that season, my Daddy started dealing in selling pills and drugs. When he and I were alone, he told me I was to keep these envelopes for him, and someone would knock on our door in the middle of the night, and I was to open the door, hand them one of the envelopes, and take an envelope from them. The next day, I would give the envelope to Daddy. This was another secret between my father and me. I was terrified to open the door and never knew what to expect, or who might be on the other side. All sorts of men showed up during the next year. One afternoon I overheard my parents talking about these tiny purple pills. My Daddy had lost all his weight taking them, and said he felt great and had lots of energy. I opened the envelopes and looked for the tiny purple pills. I took one and swallowed it before school. I didn't eat all day, and when I came home that night after work, I wasn't a bit sleepy. I felt extremely anxious and somewhat dizzy but didn't want anyone to know. I took one each day for the next 10 days and lost 12 pounds. The only thing I ingested each day was an order of fries in the afternoon with a Dr. Pepper. On the eleventh morning, I stepped into the shower and the room began to spin. I tried to grab the shower door but fell forward and blacked out. I don't know how much time had passed before mother found me. I dared not admit what I had done. I certainly didn't take tiny purple pills after that day.

More and more, Daddy began to create ways for Mother to take the boys and leave, so that we would be home alone. I was a young woman now, and he no longer wanted to be crammed in a car and parked off in the trees with the possibility of being caught. Daddy would look through his stack of pornographic magazines, and then come to my room. My head was filled with so much confusion about where my life had ended up at this point. When Daddy left my room that day, I asked God if He saw what just happened? I sobbed on my bed and apologized for asking. It was challenging to stay positive. I heard many messages that we must not question God or doubt

His promises. I so wanted to be obedient, so I wouldn't miss my miracle. There seemed to be this centrifugal force drawing me in and down toward despair. God was the only one I could talk to about my situation, and I was afraid of saying how I really felt to Him!

The school year was ending, and I was holding on for the day I would board the train and spend the summer in Alabama, where I would be reunited with my brother, Michael, and visit all my church friends there. The weather was in the upper 60's just two days before I left for Alabama. My parents had taken the boys and said they would be gone for the day. I put on a sleeveless shirt, a skirt, and rubbed down with baby oil hoping to tan, burn, or anything to show I had been in the sun. I had been out for 30 minutes or so when I heard the back door open and my father say, "Get in here and get me something to drink". Why was he home? I thought they were gone for the day. I looked in the driveway and our car was gone. "Where's mother?", I asked with a sick feeling inside that he planned all of this. "She brought me back and she took the boys with her." "Get in here". I didn't know how long he had been home, but long enough to spread pornographic magazines across the foot of the bed that were opened to scandalous images of

"I TOLD YOU I'LL KILL YOUR MOTHER AND YOU", HE SAID. I LOOKED DOWN AT THE FLOOR AND MUMBLED, "YOU ALREADY KILLED ME".

men and women. The room was charged with evil and perversion. "Oh, my Lord, is this where he is getting his ideas and his urges?", I said to myself. I stood at the door with his drink in my hand and extended toward him. He rolled his eyes around and fixed them on the bed. I put his drink on the dresser and started walking back toward the door, holding my robe tightly together. Again, he said, "Get over here." "No, Daddy," said I. "I told you I'll kill your mother and you", he said. I looked down at the floor and mumbled, "You already killed me". He came back with, "I swear on my mother it will be the last time". I just kept on walking out the bedroom door and outside to the back yard. Being a Saturday, I feared what he might do after drinking that day, or the next. But Monday morning came, and I was on a train to Alabama. The long train ride was filled with both revisiting the innumerable moments of my life and dissociating until I could once again hear the horse's gallop coming for me. Was my dream a true possibility?

A geographical change can be so refreshing. Returning to the smells of the South brought back fond and frightening memories. Reuniting with family was comforting. The week passed swiftly, and we were off to youth camp on Saturday. Being the summer before my senior year, I was in the Senior camp. There was a Jr. camp at the bottom of the hill. All the buzz was over an evangelist that would be sharing his personal testimony at Junior Camp on Thursday night. His name was Gary Smith. Gary Smith? Could it be the Gary Smith that I used to see at church events when I was 10? He sang right after my brother and me at the district convention when I wore the white dress and Michael's sport coat. He was cute and played the guitar. I remember he had on a white shirt and a black bolo. Well, he was driving his own car back then, and probably didn't even know I was alive. He had lived the past 7 years singing in a rock group and traveling the southeast with the Rolling Stones, The Turtles, and other groups doing concerts in the mid-late sixties. He had lived with an addiction to drugs, and had even overdosed multiple times, which left him nearly dead and hospitalized. He was arrested at one point, for pushing drugs, and was supposed to serve decades in prison for the crime. However, as he would captivatingly tell, he cried out from his jail cell, "If you are real, God, please help me out of this and I will give my life to you forever". If God could change his life and make something great of it, perhaps He could make something of mine.

Surprisingly enough, I didn't see Gary Smith once until the Thursday night service. When praise and worship ended, the camp director didn't give much introduction, which made it a bit suspenseful. The room was crowded, and I ended up in the back. When they turned the service over to him, things got extremely quiet, for a room of over 100 teenagers. I moved from my chair and stood along the back wall. I could see he was taking his shiny guitar from a velvet-lined case and having some difficulty getting the strap hooked around his head. He pulled a chair over and placed one foot on the chair and propped the guitar on his knee. He looked up as if someone was watching from above, and began to strum and sing, "I don't know what I'd do, I don't know what I'd do, I don't know what I'd do without the Lord . . . When I look around and see how good He's been to me, then I just don't know what I'd do without the Lord." His voice was like Kenny Rogers, smooth and with perfect pitch. He had a great touch on the guitar as well. But, as he continued singing, tears began to roll down his cheeks and onto his white shirt. Right at that moment, I felt safety and love for the first time in the presence of a man. I thought to myself, "I could marry someone like this". As quickly as the thought entered, I began to reason that he was more than five years older than me, and I was only 16. He never noticed me back then, so why would he notice me now?

The song ended with a sobering and tender silence in the room. He took 45 minutes telling unimaginable stories of his life as a drug user, pusher, and mostly as a wayward and rebellious son of a preacher man. He concluded by inviting people to come forward to give their heart to Jesus, and for prayer. I knelt behind everyone to get a closer look. Cupid's arrow pierced my heart. It seemed natural to be thinking of God and him at the same time. I had been used to pushing one out, because they didn't seem to fit together. The spiritual and the natural seemed in harmony; heaven touching earth and earth touching heaven.

The next day, Gary was with another girl for lunch and dinner. She was very pretty and had dark hair. I figured I wasn't his type. However, after church that night, we ended up in line together at the snack shack. He started a conversation and told me he remembered me singing when I was a little girl. I blushed with embarrassment that he referred to me as "a little girl". He told me his mother loved to hear me and my brother Michael sing, and that she even had our record. He asked what I would be doing for summer. I told him I was going to Florida to be the guest music at my uncle's church for a 10 night revival. "That's so weird man, he said with a nod to his hippie days. "I'm going to Florida too and I am going to be the evangelist for 10 nights in Panama City". It turned out that he was going to be the evangelist, and I was going to be the guest music for my Uncle Edward and Aunt Joyce in Panama City.

The revival started on Wednesday, and I took the bus from Birmingham to Panama City on Saturday. My uncle sent Gary to pick me up from the bus stop. I wasn't prepared for that. You see, I had naturally curly hair, and the bus wasn't air conditioned and my hair was tousled in every direction imaginable. When I saw it was Gary coming to pick me up, I burst into tears. I couldn't put my feelings into words. Perhaps it was being alone in a car with a man and thinking he could read my thoughts. He spoke comforting words by moving the conversation to the great services they had been having the past three nights. We arrived at my Uncle Edward and Aunt Joyce's soon, and it was time to get ready for church. The service went well. I noticed a very attractive woman about 20 years old in the congregation. She was the surfer type with platinum blonde hair to her waist, and a deep dark tan. Miniskirts were the thing in 1969, and she wore them well. I stood at the back door after church and overheard the young woman asking her mother to leave and that she would find a ride home. I didn't think much of it, but she went right up to Gary and asked if he could give her a ride. "Good 'ole Gary" was willing to oblique. When he pulled back in the yard of the parsonage, I had already gone to my room. The windows were opened, as it was late June and smoldering hot. He walked up to my window, and we talked a few minutes, and then said goodnight. He gave me a grin that seemed to speak louder than words. Could he be reading that I was a bit jealous?

The days were filled with study and prayer for Gary. I went to the church and practiced music during the day. Before church that night, Brother Smith (that's what we called Gary) asked me if I wanted to get a hot dog and a coke after church. I tried to stall around casually but blurted out "Yes!" instead. I don't think I have ever tried to be so spiritual as that night in church. My only comparison to my thoughts that evening were those from dissociative thoughts and dreams from the past. But why would I want to be in a field of daisies when I could be right here, in this beautiful place on the outside of my inward world?

India. https://www.britannica.com/ biography/Jawaharlal-Nehru

CHAP 10
AN ENGAGING SEASON

"THE ONLY ONE WHO COULD EVER REACH ME
WAS THE SON OF A PREACHER MAN
THE ONLY BOY WHO COULD EVER TEACH ME
WAS THE SON OF A PREACHER MAN
YES, HE WAS, YES, HE WAS, OOH,
  LORD KNOWS HE WAS"

"Son of a Preacher Man" is a song written and composed by American songwriters John Hurley and Ronnie Wilkins and recorded by British singer Dusty Springfield in September 1968 for the album Dusty in Memphis. Copyright Sony/ATV Music Publishing LLC

Revival fires were certainly ablaze in Panama City, Florida. The small church barely seated 200 people, and tonight would certainly leave some people standing. Gary was telling his testimony, and I would be hearing it for the second time. When service began, the ushers had opened the windows and put speakers out in the parking lot. People stood outside looking in, parked in their cars, and stood along the back wall of the church. Someone had called the local newspaper and stirred much interest in this former "rock 'n roll drug addict turned preacher". Gary was one of the first radical conversions, from that era, to have an instantaneous recovery from addiction to drugs, alcohol, and nicotine. People just couldn't get enough of this miraculous narrative from desperation to destiny. I was as captivated as the first time, and even more so. The prayer time was longer than usual, as many wanted to talk personally with Gary and have him pray for their own private addictions. Service concluded and it was time for us to go to "Jake's" for a hotdog and coke. Gary drove a baby blue Riviera with bucket seats. As an evangelist traveling from city to city, his clothes hung on a steel bar stretched across the back seat. I was impressed so far. After eating and mostly small talk, we drove back to the house and parked the car close to the front door. We rolled the windows down and talked about our desires to spend our lives working for the Lord. He was amazed that I had lived my whole life serving God, and never wanted anything less. My arm was resting on the passenger window, and his resting on the driver's window. There was no romantic conversation, but the atmosphere was filled with love no less. At one point, he pointed his thumb toward the clothes hanging in the back seat and said, "How would you like your clothes to be hanging there with mine?" I answered, "I really would". That's how we became engaged. There wasn't a kiss to seal the deal, or even a handheld between us. We said goodnight and spent the rest of the week dreaming and planning our future together.

I called my mother that weekend and told her I was planning to be married, and it was quite a shock. I decided I wouldn't tell her if Daddy was home. I would leave that up to Mother. When I got back to my grandmother's, my mother called and said I wasn't allowed to get married and didn't have their approval unless I graduated from high school. With only one year left in school, I now had an idea of setting a date for the wedding. I told my parents I was staying in Alabama for my senior year and that I would come to visit during Christmas. My Grandparents asked me to serve as their youth pastor, and to play the piano for church. Sometime in the fall I decided I should tell Gary some things about my past. It didn't seem fair that he was traveling the country sharing his personal testimony, and I was keeping mine from him. He interpreted the conversation to physical abuse. I wasn't strong enough to talk about the facts. But, at any rate, he became depressed and troubled in a way that caused me to regret having told him. He soon soothed my concerns by saying he felt helpless about all that had happened and unable to fix it. Once I saw his painful reaction, I made a conscious decision to spare the details and we moved forward.

The week before Christmas, we invited my cousin Donna Gaye to be a chaperone and take a road trip to Indiana to visit my family. I was shaking and shivering inside as we walked up the freshly shoveled sidewalk to the house. The snow lay delicately on the roof, shrubs, and ground. Daddy's car was in the driveway. I could feel the "golf ball" blocking my throat. Mother and the boys attacked me with hugs, but Daddy didn't come in right away. I introduced Gary to the three of them. Then, Daddy came down the hall and stopped shy of the living room and nodded his head up and down. They didn't shake hands or talk to one another. I approached Daddy and gave him a brief hug. I could feel his hands trembling. He went back to the back of the house. I had to go to the bathroom and saw Daddy standing in the bathroom and he ripped a hand towel completely apart with his teeth and said, "that's MY girl". I quickly ran back to the living room and sat apart from Gary. I don't know why I didn't just sit by him and hold his hand. The memories and fears of all the years in that house was overwhelming me and time stood still. We made it through the next three days and exchanged presents with the family. The boys really seemed to warm up to Gary. I was counting down the minutes until we could get back in the car, close the door, and leave.

1970 rolled around and our wedding day would be May 30, 1970. Two weeks before the wedding, I went to see a doctor in Birmingham for my first physical examination. He was an elderly man in his final year of practice before retirement. He had been the Smith's family doctor for years, and even delivered Gary. During the exam, I whimpered and whispered it felt uncomfortable. He started laughing, slapped me on the butt and said, "Well, little lady, you better get used to this." I left the office feeling such shame that I wouldn't tell what he did until years later. I graduated May 26, on a Tuesday night. My parents drove down from Indiana the day before graduation and stayed through until the wedding. I was asked to sing a solo for my graduation, and felt honored to represent my class. My Daddy started drinking once graduation was over and only four days until I married. I avoided my Daddy at all opportunities. I didn't know what he might say if we were alone together. Gary drove down from Birmingham Friday night for the rehearsal. We all waited and waited for Daddy to arrive. When he walked in the church, he was disheveled and smelled of cigarettes and liquor. His eyes were bloodshot as he came up to me and said, "I'm gonna' take you back to Indiana. I'm going to come and get you". He didn't stay for the rehearsal. Some thought it was so "cute" that he didn't want his daughter to get married. I didn't tell Gary what Daddy had said. I didn't want anything to ruin my plans. I made a mad dash for my grandmother's as soon as I could and packed my suitcase. I asked my aunt Annette if I could spend the night with her. Her house was far out in the country, and I was in fear my father would act on his word. I didn't sleep at all and instead sat staring out the bedroom window in torment that he might spoil our plans. I was too upset to eat breakfast on my wedding day. My mother picked me up and drove me to town to buy a set of luggage for my wedding present. I had a bag of popcorn and a Dr. Pepper for lunch. Daddy was gone when we went back to my grandmother's to get ready. We all loaded up and left for the church two hours before the ceremony.

When it was time for the service, the singer began singing "I Love You Truly", as the wedding party took their positions in the front of the church. I was standing on the porch of the church when Daddy pulled abruptly into the parking lot. He was drinking and smoking. He smashed his cigarette in the gravel, walked up the steps of the church, and walked me down the aisle. His arm was trembling, as was mine. I made no eye contact with him. I kept my eyes straight ahead to my husband to be, or at least that was my prayer. The ceremony was a blur until the minister pronounced us husband and wife. I was Mrs. Gary Smith forever! We left the reception in the pouring rain. My wedding dress was dragged through the mud in the parking lot and served as describing how I felt about being presented as a bride. I didn't know if I could ever tell my husband about all the events I had experienced, and I decided I never would.

For the first time in my life, I began to sneak out from the life in my head to view the one on the outside. My husband loved me fully and completely. I felt safe and covered by him, and knew he was committed for a lifetime. We didn't have a place to live at first and ended up staying with his parents in Birmingham the first summer of our married life. Gary preached within a hundred-mile radius of Birmingham, and I worked as a secretary at a metal products company. By September, I quit my job because our travels were now taking us from one state to another. We lived out of a suitcase and stayed in different pastors' homes the first year and a half. In September of 1971, I had a miscarriage. I was in fear that it was related to my childhood situation. I was too frightened to mention it to the doctors, and Gary had also been told he would risk fathering a child, due to his abuse and duration of taking drugs for so many years. Neither of us wanted to discuss what could have caused the miscarriage with anyone. I had begun to dream a little about having a child, and those dreams were now gone, and it was a lonely and painful time for Gary and me. We took a week off from traveling to recover.

Gary, my brother Michael, and I toured the nation in revival crusades and anti-drug campaigns in colleges and high schools. Gary's rock 'n roll days of concerts and pushing drugs, and a few overdoses landed him in jail facing a 20 year prison sentence. It was miraculously overturned, and he was pardoned with the caveat that he would speak in high schools and colleges across the nation on the dangers of drug addiction. By Christmas of 1971, I was pregnant with our son Jeffrey. The doctor advised me to travel as little as possible until Jeffrey was born. During that Christmas holiday, there was a tragedy about 90 miles from Birmingham, Alabama that involved a pastoral family we knew in Hamilton, Alabama. The teenage son was driving the family of five and collided head on with another automobile. The teenage son, young baby daughter and the father were all killed. The Alabama state overseer of our denomination approached my husband to serve as interim pastor until August of the next year, which was my due date. We had no training for being lead pastors, but it seemed to be a great fit for the church's healing, and for our circumstance.

I always had anxiety attacks when it was time for pelvic examinations. I could feel my blood pressure rising and the "golf ball" in my throat. Each doctor I saw would tell me to relax, which amplified my anxiety. I must admit, I tranced out in dissociation a few times when I felt out of control. I didn't make the connection at first between the invasiveness of the exam and my history. The PTSD was overwhelming, which triggered the dissociation. For more information on the subject, you can learn more from the book, "The Single Guide to Complex Trauma and Dissociation: What it is and How to Help (Simple Guides)" by Betsy de Thierry. I also suffered from Hyperemesis Gravidarum, which is continuous nausea during pregnancy. Most women experience some sort of adverse response to smells or the sight of certain things early on in pregnancy. Some even experience nausea for the first few weeks. However, others continue vomiting, losing weight, and becoming dizzy and dehydrated. I fit in the latter category with all my pregnancies. I was vomiting on the way to the hospital to deliver.

One of the greatest days ever was when our son was born. He arrived on August 7, 1972, weighing 7lbs. 12oz., and born at 7:02 p.m. We named him Jeffrey Allen Smith. The name Allen had passed from my husband's father to Gary, and now to Jeffrey. It would later be passed to our son Tyler, and to our grandson Jude Allen. Jeffrey was the beautiful expression of pure love between the two of us. He was beautiful, innocent, gentle and fresh from the hands of God. We had no insurance or extra money when Jeffrey came along, and the hospital was across the Alabama state line in Mississippi. We had no relatives or close friends living near us and no one to ask or answer questions we might have. When my labor was induced, I became anxious and fearful. Thankfully, the doctors back then highly sedated women and I was dissociating and hallucinating for hours. I suppose it is the closest I would ever come to knowing about a drug-induced episode. In the delivery room, I was so sedated that the doctor smacked me and said, "Push, Push Mrs. Smith". I replied, "Wait a minute I know I had a baby already. Is it a girl or a boy?" He seemed to be speaking over a loud system with reverb on his voice as he once again said, "Push, push". I have zero recollection from that moment until I was back in my room and the nurse awakened me to place my baby in my arms. I didn't want anyone to know I was completely zoned out from the entire experience. I had completely missed a very traumatic moment when the nurse took Jeffrey and held the bloody newborn up to the window to show the new father, and Gary burst through the doors to the delivery room, grabbed his son and started running down the hallway. They screamed for him to stop, which he did. He thought something was wrong with our baby. As I stated earlier, we didn't know what to expect. It was 9:30-10 p.m. when they brought a tray of food to our room. We were broke and shared the meal between us. It was better than being in a 5-star restaurant that night with our new little family. Gary didn't have enough gas to drive the 45-50 miles back to Hamilton, and so we propped a shoe in the exit door, and Gary sneaked back into my bed for the night. The nurse was kind-hearted to our situation and didn't report us to her superiors.

When Jeffrey was only 10 days old, we put a bassinet in the back seat, our clothes in the trunk, and headed back on the road for crusades and assemblies. After four months of moving everything in and out of the pastor's homes, we bought a travel trailer to pull behind an older light blue Cadillac that we had purchased. When Christmas came, we split our two weeks off between Gary's parents and mine. It was extremely awkward to spend the night at my parents, even though they had now moved back to Alabama from Indiana. I tried to avoid any moments alone with my father. Gary noticed something about me and called me into the bedroom. "Why are you holding your head down and not speaking up when you talk?" Those comments were all I needed to see the profound affect the environment was holding on me. I had become the broken little girl all over again and felt trapped and limited in both posture and conversation. Mealtime was the most difficult, as I had to sit in proximity with Daddy. By now, I had told Gary a few details from my childhood that infuriated him, and even convinced him to buy a gun. I could see my Daddy cutting his eyes at Gary when he thought no one was observing, and watching Gary keep a close eye on him. Even though I was an adult, the broken child in me wanted everything to be okay. I realized I was ready to start dealing with reality.

I was glad when Christmas was over, and we were back to our own little family. My brother Michael joined us a few months later, and we relished traveling the nation together and seeing the beauty of God's creation across the U.S.A. By the time Jeffrey was 8 months old, he had traveled to Alabama, Tennessee, Georgia, Mississippi, Louisiana, Texas, New Mexico, Arizona, Nevada, California, Washington, Oregon, and Juarez, Mexico. Our crusades were always ten days long, from Wednesday until the following Sunday. We used Monday, Tuesday and Wednesday to travel to our next location. Jeffrey was a perfect child, and he sang along and banged along in rhythm from his jumper seat every night in church. It was certainly a foretelling of greater things to come.

The year seemed to pass with the speed of light and it was another Christmas. Jeffrey was 16 months old, and we were at my parents' for Christmas on a bitter cold morning. Both sets of parents lived in houses that had grills in the floor that provided and distributed heat. Jeffrey, only 16 months old was barefoot and stepped on the fiery grill and froze as he began screaming. I ran quickly and scooped him up to find red grill marks on his little feet and we headed straight for the emergency room, which was seven or so miles away. My parents followed behind in their car. My Dad had been out all night and had just come home. He and mother drove in one car, and Gary, Jeffrey and I rode behind them in ours. When we arrived at the ER, we filled out the papers and were told to take a seat in the over-crowded waiting room. Jeffrey was inconsolable, to say the least. I held him, rocked him, sang to him, prayed over him and tried everything to distract him. Finally, my Daddy got up and went down the hall toward the examination room, took a pistol from his pocket, and pointed it at the ER doctor and said, "You're gonna' see my grandson, and you're gonna' see him right now, do you hear me?" I remembered that tone because I had heard it for years telling me what I was gonna' do. The ER Doctor immediately emerged from the hall and said, "Jeffrey Smith? Jeffrey Smith?" No security or authorities were ever alerted. The doctor just treated Jeffrey, and we all quietly left the hospital. It was unbelievable how Daddy was still getting away with things.

We continued traveling until late summer of 1974. I had suffered two miscarriages since Jeffrey and had just gotten pregnant again.

We were offered the pastorate of a church in Olathe, Kansas. We stayed a year, and our beautiful daughter, Stacey Janea', was born. When she was one month old, we moved across town to Kansas City, Kansas and pastored there for a year. Gary didn't realize until years later that I struggled so much with the past and was restless spending too

> **I THOUGHT I WAS HOLDING A PIECE OF HEAVEN, NOT KNOWING THAT IN A FEW SHORT YEARS I WOULD BE HOLDING THE THING I FEARED THE MOST.**

much time in one place. I always managed to talk him into getting away and changing the scenery. When Stacey was two, we moved to Orlando, Florida. For the first time ever, I thought I was holding a piece of heaven, not knowing that in a few short years I would be holding the thing I feared the most.

- *When Survivors Give Birth: Understanding and Healing the Effects of Early Sexual Abuse on Childbearing Women*
- Simkin, Penny and Phyllis H. Klaus. Seattle: Classic Day, 2011. Print.

Posted in: Abuse and Violence, Induction and Labor, Nursing, Obstetrics, Women's Health

CHAP 11
THE GUN CHANGES HANDS

"WHEN YOUR DAY IS LONG
AND THE NIGHT, THE NIGHT IS YOURS ALONE
WHEN YOU'RE SURE YOU'VE HAD ENOUGH
OF THIS LIFE, WELL HANG ON
DON'T LET YOURSELF GO, CAUSE EVERYBODY CRIES
EVERYBODY HURTS SOMETIMES"

Everybody Hurts, Songwriters: Buck, peter Lawrence, Stipe, john Michael, Berry, william Thomas, Mills, michael Edward. Copyright Night Garden Music

It's one thing to have a weapon pointing at you, and quite another to be the one doing the pointing. Movies portray the act as effortless and deliberate. Pow! It can end a life so suddenly. Just a few short years ago, a beloved family member thought pulling the trigger was an answer to his complicated life. He had struggled in his adult life with alcohol, which cost his marriage. His youngest child was involved in a tragic accident that left her severely impaired and unable to function on her own. He had spent his inheritance on frivolous living, and pulling the trigger seemed the only solution to his maddening world.

I would love to be the one to say, "how could someone sink to such depths?" However, I too, was in such a pit in the early 1980's. After years of evangelizing and pastoring, Gary and I had ended up singing in a club in Orlando, Florida for a living. At the time, we had no appointments or assignments with any church organization, and we were told of an audition at the Kahler Hotel in Orlando, Florida. They were looking for a duo to sing dinner music from 6-10 p.m., Tuesday through Saturday. The only problem was that we only knew Christian music. With no time to waste, we bought a 45 rpm of John Denver singing, "Take Me Home Country Road". We got the job on Monday, and they asked us to start the next night. We scurried to the record shops and worked around the clock to learn 6 songs for the grand opening. We named ourselves, "Heart and Soul". I suppose it was up for grabs on who was the heart, and who was the soul. The humorous part of it all is that God's gifts and anointing on our life flowed over to everything we played or sang.

People would get teary-eyed and feel chills as we sang John Denver, Roberta Flack, or even Cindy Lauper. It paid great money, and we had two beautiful children to care for. We wanted the best for them . . . music lessons, sports, dance, and acting were all a part of the opportunities we wanted to provide for our children. These extra-curricular activities were expensive, and we were willing to work hard to have them. We saw great potential in our children. We made affiliations with other artists during this time. Gary also took a day job working on the railroad in a hard-labor setting amidst the hot Florida sun. It was the most challenging time of our lives. I had only been involved in church work and ministry up until then. It seemed I had somehow forsaken my calling. There was something disparaging about the environment that brought back sensory stimuli revisiting my childhood. There was

I FELT I HAD BECOME A MECHANICAL AND WELL-TRAINED ROBOT OUTWARDLY, WITH A BROKEN CHILD TRYING TO HOLD THE GAME CONTROLLER INWARDLY.

a powerful pairing of smells, liquor, temperatures, cigarettes, and events that seemed to shower over me and call out the broken child from within to the broken woman I had become. I felt I had become a mechanical and well-trained robot outwardly, with a broken child trying to hold the game controller inwardly.

The human body is a masterful machine containing innumerable components that work holistically to maintain our functionality for existence, expression, and fulfillment. Two important parts of our brain, the hippocampus and the amygdala are involved with memory. The hippocampus works to stamp and date an event, while the amygdala attaches the emotions and feelings to the event. So, for example, a person may have had a picnic in a peach orchard as a child. In the present, they may smell a peach, and recall the event, with all the details, including it to have occurred on July 4, 1988. However, when there is fear or trauma that reaches a certain threshold, the hippocampus fails to put the stamp and date on the event. The amygdala continues to operate without a stamp and date, leaving the person feeling as though the event is occurring in the present. Suppose that same person instead, suffered a gunshot wound in 10th grade, at the hands of a terrorist while in high school. In the present, they may smell gun powder and there is no stamp and date on the event, only fear and feelings that the event is occurring in the here and now.

As the combination of certain triggers combined, I was in the trauma all over again inwardly. Depression settled into a new degree with consuming dread and hopelessness. I would tape black garbage bags over the windows as soon as the children left for school and spend the days reliving the past over and over. I suppose I had just begun to come face to face with my history. Why? What? How? It was too much for me.

To compound the issue, I had begun phone conversations with someone else that was also occupying my thoughts and became a distraction from reality. While the conversations were not sexual in nature, I was feeling an inappropriate connection, and found myself wondering when I would be able to speak to them again. In hindsight, I now see that the enemy of our souls would love to take every opportunity to pull us aside from our destiny and purpose in exchange for a substitute. Betrayal can be emotional as well as physical. When our thoughts are turned toward another, and away from our spouse, it is a form of adultery of the heart and a betrayal of our vows. My true destiny and purpose were right in front of me, and I had already invested 13 years toward fulfilling it. My husband felt a sense of accomplishment, despite the adverse conditions from working two jobs. He was determined to take our family to the next level, and I had somehow lost sight of my purpose.

One event brought everything to a standing halt in my mind. As we headed home after dinner that evening, I so wanted to talk and just clear the air, but my history of guilt and shame metaphorically cupped my mouth and silenced me. The night was restless and filled with vain imagination. I was creating aggrandized scenarios that could jeopardize the one true person I ever really loved, and that honorably loved me. I awakened at 6 a.m. the following morning, and told my husband there was something I simply must disclose, and ensued with the detailed accounts of phone conversations between that person and myself. His countenance revealed he was both hurt and disappointed, as was I. Long after my last words were spoken, he carefully but firmly replied that I had broken the trust between us and that it would require time to heal. He read a scripture, which I don't recall, prayed over me, and said he would have to take responsibility for protecting our family in the future. I was skeptical of such drastic measures at the time, but with hindsight, I see that it saved our lives from destruction.

I would love to say we took an upward climb from that day, but honestly, I sank deeper into depression. By now, I was living less as a reflection of my own soul, and more by the expectations of others. I began to overplay my love, actions, and devotion to a fault. Oddly enough, it seemed to work for everyone else. It was a trying task to stay in character. My unhealthy self was spiraling deeper into regret and shame. My ever-present thought was being responsible for breaking the trust in our home. I had survived 13 years of physical, emotion and sexual abuse at the hands of another! SIN IS BLIND! Sin fails to show you the tainted future, and the losses resulting from its grip. The consequentiality of sin was surmounting beyond my ability to maintain.

Robin Williams, a well-known comedian, and award-winning actor took his life in August of 2014. The world of entertainment was completely stunned at the news. An anchorman with a syndicated news station commented, "It's hard to imagine, isn't it? And yet, something inside you is so horrible or you're such a coward or whatever the reason that you decide that you must end it." Professionals in the field of psychology quickly reacted to the comments. A research psychologist, Jesse Bering, wrote an article for Scientific American. This publication is one that told his own story of suicidal thoughts, as well as provided further research on the topic. Bering stated, "In considering peoples' motivations for killing themselves, it is essential to recognize that most suicides are driven by a flash flood of strong emotions, not rational, philosophical thoughts in which the pros and cons are evaluated critically." He referred to Roy Baumeister's model from a 1990 Psychology Review paper "Suicide as Escape from the Self." Baumeister, Florida State psychologist, states there is a sequence of cognitive patterns that possibly lead to suicide. These are, and I quote:

1) "Failing to meet your standards for yourself. Suicidal ideations are not respectful of socioeconomic status, education, gender, prominence, popularity. In fact, among those with higher grades and higher expectations, the risk can be greater.

2) Condemning yourself for failing to meet the standards. We are, indeed, our worse critics. When we fail, we are the first to recognize and the first to criticize ourselves. This refers to all the feelings of shame, guilt, inadequacy, humiliation, rejection, and worthlessness. Feeling painfully self-aware (this refers to comparing yourself to others and trying to escape the self that you dislike.) Suicide seems easier than working through the fact that you have missed the mark or avoided dealing with behaviors that have led to the current situation.

3) Experience "negative affect," or extremely difficult emotions (with loss through relationships, death, or divorce, possible clinical depression will dull positive events and magnify the negative ones.

4) Trying to avoid meaningful thoughts. Suicidal people may engage in "cognitive deconstruction," to keep from feelings that might be meaningful or change their minds. The deep desire in all of God's creation is to find that ray of hope and allow it to surface as a mechanism for moving beyond despair. Suicidal ideations block the possibility of discovering any hope.

5) Dis-inhibition is about abandoning the idea of wanting to live, feeling obligated to family, or wondering about long-term consequences."

He concluded the article with these words: "Physical or sexual abuse as a child, combat exposure, and domestic abuse can also 'prep' the individual for the physical pain associated with suicidal behavior."

The gun . . . . I remembered my father held it to my head and threatened to kill my mother and me. It would have been quick, and it would have changed everything. This time, the gun changes hands. In desperation, I took a loaded gun and put it to my temple and within seconds I fired and felt a paralyzing sensation soaring through my entire being. I watched what appeared to be slow motion as the gun extended from my hand toward the floor. The explosion seemed to intensify as I quickly released the gun from my hand and reached for my head, expecting to feel blood. Still, very dissociated from reality, I began to realize the gun, in fact, had exploded toward the floor, firing into a basket of folded laundry. The holes in the towels and underwear were reminders that one quick pull of a trigger can change everything. There was no life left in me at that moment, but I could hear a voice afterwards speaking to me that said, "Life is coming".

My husband returned from work, and I owned up to attempting suicide and felt it was the only solution and that everyone would be better off without me. Deep inside I knew I had to take ownership of where I had allowed myself to drift, but I just couldn't figure out a way to start.

The next day, my husband vowed to God that things were going to change. Over the next two weeks, he went on a complete fast from food, and only ingested liquids. It was humbling to observe his sacrifice for our marriage and family. He came home from work one day with a stack of Christian books and tossed them on the bed, as he pleaded with me to please read these. I looked for the thinnest book in the stack. I was too mentally expended to think of reading a thick book. It turned out to be, "Favor, the Road to Success," by Bob Buess. Here are the opening words of the introduction:

"This message has been in my spirit for about eight years. I have been ministering it to others with dramatic changes coming to pass in their lives as a result. This message will have a powerful influence upon your life - if you will allow it to minister to your spirit. Many people, due to childhood experiences, bad situations in marriage, or other reasons, withdraw into a shell of fear, frustration, or negativism. This truth will help such people realize the Lord Jesus, who is within them, to have a full, exciting, and exuberant life. These people will begin living with excitement, expecting to meet happy people. Favor will begin to flow. You will reap what you sow. Expect good things to happen, and these will be the things that start happening to you. Thoughts are the beginning of reality. The Holy Spirit plants good thoughts into your mind. As you meditate upon these positive thoughts, they are transferred to your spirit. Once these thoughts are planted in your spirit, life begins to grow. Your life is controlled by the things that you place in your spirit, by way of your thought pattern."

God seemed to give Bob Buess the very words I needed. All my life, no one spoke over me or helped me believe I made a difference in a positive way. I felt as though I was plowed ground, receiving seeds of life that immediately began to spring forth. Jesus said, "The words that I speak unto you, they are spirit, and they are life" (John 6:63). Speak His words, speak the Scriptures, because the word of God is life. Hebrews 4:12 (NASB) affirms this: "The word of God is living and active." I began to test that idea over the next few weeks. I knew this in my heart long before I felt it in my body and life.

It was during this awkward time between that I heard a knock at my front door. I could hear people talking to one another rather loudly, mixed with joy and laughter. I hesitantly opened the door and saw three people wearing jogging suits and gym shoes. They asked if they could enter, and I opened the door fully and they took their own positions about the living room. One of them, the shortest and somewhat rotund, bounced down onto the loveseat, and swung one leg over the arm. The other two laughed and chuckled. One rolled her eyes at me as if to say, "There she goes again", referring to the one that plopped herself down on the chair. The taller one picked up the newspaper and they all addressed the front page articled of a major accident that had occurred. They were speaking of intervening in a near death that would have taken the life of the driver. I cannot recall much more of the specific conversation, but suddenly I blurted out, "I know why you're here . . . you're here to spread joy and to lift my sadness". They laughed the louder, and I put great effort into resisting their joy. I was rather cynical, and wasn't buying into some quick fix, but despite my efforts to hold back, I began to laugh. I laughed until tears were streaming, and my side was aching. They said it was time to go now and got up and I walked them to the front door. My head longed to deny, but my heart confirmed I had been visited by angels from heaven. They were sent to minister to me. Psalms 91:11,12. "For He will command his angels concerning you to guard you in all your ways, they will lift you up in their hands, so that you will not strike your foot against a stone."

My idea of having a visitation by angels would have been halos, harps, and pixie glitter. There was no question in my heart that angels had responded to a heavenly assignment. I was their assignment. During that period, I identified with Gideon in the book of Judges. (Judges 6) God had previously delivered Israel from Egyptian bondage and encouraged them to go forward and not fear the Amorites (their enemies), but they didn't listen. Now they were surrounded by Midianites and hiding in caves and forts in fear. God sent an angel to Gideon and said, "God is with you, O mighty warrior!" Without hesitation,

Gideon basically said, "Really? If God is with us, why has all of this happened to us? Where are the miracles, signs, and wonders our family told us about? Here we are, just turned over to the Midianites. You've got the wrong guy. Check me out. My clan is the weakest in Manasseh and look at me! I'm the runt of the bunch." God said to him, "I will be with you. Just believe me, and you're going to defeat Midian as one man. Gideon, perhaps much like me with the visitation from the three angels, replied, "I tell you what, do me a favor. Give me a sign to back up what you are saying. And don't leave until I come back and bring my gift." Gideon returned with a prepared goat, broth, and unleavened bread. The angel told him to put the meat and bread on a rock and to pour the broth over it. When Gideon obeyed, the angel stretched the tip of a stick he was holding and touched the meat and the bread. Fire broke out and burned up the meat and bread as the angel of God also slipped out of sight. Gideon then knew it was the angel of God. The rest of the story reveals Gideon's personal path to faith and victory. His initial response to the angel of the Lord was "You've got the wrong guy". In the end his victory cry is, "For the Lord and for Gideon" (Judges 7:18)

Our greatest confidence builder is God. He speaks over us with words of victory and greatness. "For I know the thoughts I think toward you, says the Lord, thoughts of peace and not of evil, to give you a future and a hope." Jeremiah 29:11. Oftentimes, we listen to what the world is saying through television, movies, social media, and pop culture. However, only God's standard is steady, enduring, and never changing. Our greatest efforts to keep up with the times and the trends leave us lacking in one area or another. Because trends and styles are ever changing, they bring with the changes great pressure to stay in the constant flow of change to be accepted and approved. While temporary acceptance may be experienced by adhering to these demands, God alone is the true source of acceptance and unconditional love.

Perhaps you have embraced a substitute while searching for a valid answer to the questions of your past. If your search has led you to a more complicated life, you might want to assess your situation. Take a glimpse back at your life prior to your poor choices. I, as Gideon, was feeling God had somehow forgotten me. Where are the miracles, the promises, and the great things we had been told God would do for all these years? These moments of doubt create a door of opportunity for sin to enter. Had "sin" shown you what the future would hold, would you still have taken its bait? Sin has one direction: DEATH. Sin might appear to bring you something you think is missing, but it is deceptive to the very core. It is corrupt and devalues every person it touches. Of course, we know "Sin" is from the evil one. It's not too late to own up to your skewed resolve and find the true answers that God has for your life. It is a risk worth taking.

I was convinced through vain imaginations that I couldn't speak out feelings and emotions that were factual. I was always punished emotionally when I spoke anything apart from perfection growing up, and I had dragged that broken child into the broken girl, and broken woman I had become. God brought authenticity and value into my life, as I could clearly see God had provided someone all along who truly loved me and cared for me. Sin blurs our vision from the truth. In John 8:31-32 Jesus was speaking to the Jews that believed in Him. "If you continue in my word, then are you my disciples indeed. And you will KNOW the Truth, and the truth will set you free." I am thankful I knew the Truth, but I wondered, "Could I ever truly be set free?"

*https://www.lancashirecare.nhs.uk/media/ Publications/Traumatic-Stress-Service/How-Trauma-Affects.pdf

CHAP 12
MEMORIES

"MEMORIES
LIGHT THE CORNERS OF MY MIND
MISTY WATERCOLOR MEMORIES
OF THE WAY WE WERE
SCATTERED PICTURES
OF THE SMILES WE LEFT BEHIND
SMILES WE GAVE TO ONE ANOTHER
FOR THE WAY WE WERE"

The Way We Were (1974), Songwriters: Marvin Hamlisch, Marilyn Bergman, Alan Bergman. Copyright Arlovol Music, Colgems-emi Music Inc., Vbzelect Publishing

Barbara Streisand's number one song in 1974 "The Way We Were" should have been written by a neuroscientist. The lyrics read: "Memories, light the corners of my mind. Misty watercolor memories of the way we were. Scattered pictures of the smiles we left behind; smiles we gave to one another for the way we were." Our brain circuitry does, in fact, light up areas of our mind when we are engaged in the process of remembering.

Have you ever wondered why we cannot choose to retain the favorable memories and discard the unwanted ones? I've wondered it for years. It took the focus of this book to conclude our lives to be a continuous flow of ups and downs, good and bad, voluntary, and involuntary. Selective memory is impossible. In fact, our adverse memories can serve a purpose to correct a current event, minimize its potency, and become an opportunity for growth in our current lives. I'm reminded of the movie Groundhog's Day, (1993) that starred Bill Murray as a meteorologist covering the annual groundhog's day festival in Pennsylvania. To his surprise, when the alarm sounded each morning, it was a repeat of the day before that continued eight years, eight months, according to the website Wolf Gnards. From a psychosocial and "Eriksonian" ego theory, Phil Conners, Murray's character, represents a man in middle adulthood, that has clearly failed to end up with the virtue of "Care".

Erikson states that a proper transition from this stage of Generativity vs. Stagnation (ages 40-65) results in being a caring person. Failing to allow this virtue to result leads to stagnation. Phil Conners is extremely stagnated at this juncture of his existence. He sees himself as the center of the universe and condescends upon everyone with who he encounters. According to Erikson: "Generativity refers to "making your mark" on the world through creating or nurturing things that will outlast an individual." Phil Conners seemed to be obsessed with nurturing himself and his needs, to the exclusion of all others. Therefore, he fell into the category of "Stagnation". He was disconnected and uninvolved in others. Should he have nurtured a "generative" attitude, he would have opened himself more to others and their wellbeing. Oddly enough, the continuous repeating of groundhog's day gave Phil Conners a chance to correct his failing to properly transition from other psychosocial stages.

Just to refresh, Erikson's Psychosocial Stages are:

1) Trust vs. Mistrust – the resulting positive virtue is HOPE (oral-sensory. Infant-under 2 years)
2) Autonomy vs. Shame- The resulting positive virtue is WILL (muscular-anal. 2 -3 years)
3) Initiative vs. Guilt – The resulting positive virtue is PURPOSE (locomotor-genital, 3-6 years)
4) Industry vs. Inferiority- The resulting positive virtue is COMPENTENCE (latency, middle childhood 7-12 years)
5) Identity vs. Role Confusion The resulting virtue is FIDELITY (adolescence, 12-19 years)
6) Intimacy vs. Isolation-The resulting positive virtue is LOVE (early adulthood 20-39 years)
7) Generativity vs. Stagnation-The resulting virtue is CARE (middle adulthood, 40-59 years) *Bill Murray
8) Ego Integrity vs. Despair -The resulting positive virtue is WISDOM (late adulthood, 60 years and above)

Bill Murray's character, unlike real life, had a chance to revisit and correct his past. He used his working memories to change the things that were obstacles in his life and embrace a better version of himself in the process. He reverted to the Identity vs. Role Confusion stage that normally occurs between the ages of 12-18, and results in the virtue of Fidelity. Fidelity occurs in the adolescent time in life that defines who we are, along with forming social and peer relationships. Fidelity is concerned with faithfulness in relationships. Murray's character came face to face with his stagnant life, and in his childish way, tried to recapture a time that had passed him by. He showed his "role confusion" in the scene where he is driving the car on the railroad, and almost kills himself. He is lacking in identity and exhibits role confusion instead.

Erikson's sixth stage: Intimacy vs. Isolation. We can assume from a psychosocial observation that Phil Conners obviously chose isolation over intimacy during this transition of development. He is lonely and alone. His failure to embrace intimacy left him isolated from love. Murray reverts to young adulthood and strives to make love with Nancy (his opposite character) by manipulating her own words and stories from the previously repeating days that have passed, using them all for his own advantage. He was more concerned with sex than intimacy. The consequence was isolation. In the "happily ever after", we would want to think he not only re-transitioned through the psychosocial stages up to the ending of the movie, but that he was able to gain the virtue of wisdom by living with integrity rather than despair, which is Erik Erikson's eighth and last stage of development.

Our brain is a creative and malleable machine, with new opportunities each day. Memories are a gift to allow us to revisit unpleasant thoughts for new interpretations and meanings, embracing those thoughts we love, cherish and long to hold onto, as well as providing snapshots of significant dates and time stamps in our lives. Many suffer depression, and even PTSD, over past traumatic memories. New research in optogenetics shows the greatest way for fear extinction to occur is through neural plasticity, which is the brain's own ability to regenerate and form new neural pathways.

God designed us for optimal operation and equipped us with abilities beyond all we could ask or imagine. Here are a few facts about memory:

- Memory begins in the womb, 20 weeks after conception.
- We are blessed with short and long-term memory. Short term memory, however, lasts only 20 or 30 seconds. (What was I just saying?)
- Memory can be visual, auditory, or tactile and is based on factors from either.
- Our storage capacity for memory is virtually limitless. (Keep learning)

- Sleep aids us in both storage and retrieval of memory. (For all you nappers)

Many people associate memory loss with aging. However, the memory loss we experience the older we get is generally because we tend to exercise our brains less as we age. Your memory can associate a scent with a certain event. A smell can trigger the memory that is associated with it. The hippocampus is mainly responsible for formation of new memories, and acts in conjunction with our olfactory sense of smell. There is something called false memory, whereby the brain exaggerates or distorts traumatic events. The mind must be exercised just as any other part of the body. Thinking about memories creates stronger links between activate neurons. We tend to retain more information we have read if it is in a strange or unique font. (this caused me to reconsider the font I had chosen for this book.)

I am notating here a few significant scriptures regarding memory and memorization that are found in the Bible.

- Proverbs 7:1 My son, keep my words, and lay up my commandments with thee.
- Proverbs 7:2. Keep my commandments, and live; and my law as the apple of thine eye.
- Proverbs 7:3. Bind them upon thy fingers, write them upon the table of thine heart.

- Isaiah 46:9 - Remember the former things of old: for I [am] God, and [there is] none else; [I am] God, and [there is] none like me,
- I Corinthians 15:1Moreover, brethren, I declare unto you the gospel which I preached unto you, which also ye have received, and wherein ye stand; 2By which also ye are saved, if ye keep in memory what I preached unto you, unless ye have believed in vain.
- Proverbs 10:7 - The memory of the just [is] blessed.
- John 14:26 - But the Comforter, [which is] the Holy Ghost, whom the Father will send in my name, he shall teach you all things, and bring all things to your remembrance, whatsoever I have said unto you.

These passages assure us we are not left alone with our memories. God has sent the Holy Spirit to equip us and assist us on our journey. For me, I now understand that a ruminating memory is in fact an opportunity for me to reassess, reanalyze, and understand myself from a fresh perspective. The worse mistake I could ever have made would be to write off every negative event of my life and fail to examine it for a new opportunity toward healing. They say elephants have the greatest memories.

Hang with me and see if you can spot the white elephant in the room.

THE WORSE MISTAKE I COULD EVER HAVE MADE WOULD BE TO WRITE OFF EVERY NEGATIVE EVENT OF MY LIFE AND FAIL TO EXAMINE IT FOR A NEW OPPORTUNITY TOWARD HEALING.

McLeod, S. A. (2018, May 03). Erik Erikson's stages of psychosocial development. Retrieved from https://www.simplypsychology.org/Erik-Erikson.html
Albert, T. (Producer), & Ramis, H. (Director). (1993). Groundhog Day. [Motion picture]. USA: Columbia TriStar Films.
Gravetter, F.J. & Forzano, L.B. (2012). Research Methods. For the Behavioral Science. Belmont, CA: Wadsworth.
Ryckman, R.M. (2008). Theories of Personality. Belmont, CA: Wadsworth. scientificamerican.com/How the Brain Purges Bad Memories
A brain circuit has been found that allows us to forget fear and anxiety/By Bret Stetka on July 31, 2015

CHAP 13
WHITE ELEPHANT IN THE ROOM

"NO ONE EVER SEEMS TO SEE
THE WHITE ELEPHANT FOLLOWING ME
THEY DON'T ACKNOWLEDGE IT EXISTS
I SEEM TO SEE WHAT OTHERS MISS
A CROWDED ROOM WITH EMPTY PEOPLE
WHO IGNORE THE RELEVANCE
OF THE WHITE ELEPHANT."

Written by Janis Smith, 2021. Copyright 2021 Janis Smith

Most of us know the idiom, "the white elephant in the room". Those who may have missed it along the way might want to know of this white elephant. It represents an obvious problem no one wants to address. Mark Twain mentions the white elephant in a story written in 1882, referring to detectives searching for an elephant that was in plain view all along. A Russian fabulist, Ivan Krylov Andreevich, in the early 1800's, also wrote about an elephant in the room in a fable entitled "The Inquisitive Man". Social settings have somewhat of a codification of social interactions that appear as a white elephant in the room when the topic is taboo. The topics are innumerable ranging from, religion, addictions, politics, race, sexual abuse, physical abuse, etc. The white elephant is easier to ignore than to acknowledge. I reached a point in life when every single space was filled with the white elephant. This white elephant accompanied me wherever I traveled. I often received a "How are you? Is everything okay?" but not once in decades did anyone address the obvious fact that I was struggling. After 10 years of college and two years of writing my dissertation, I had great expectations that some huge event would move the white elephant.

What seemed to be great achievements by some standards left me sharing everything with a white elephant.

The greatest and most stellar example of the white elephant became my greatest challenge each time I visited home and in the presence of my father. I was very guarded to keep my distance from any opportunities to be alone, or to have my father alone with my children. It was a difficult task, at the very least. He always had a loud and humorous approach with crowds, and especially children. My children thought he was hilarious and animated with his country accent, jokes, and stories. He mostly wore work jumpsuits and overalls from the time my children were born. He had moved back to his roots in Alabama, and just became, well, a "country bumpkin" as they call it. I recall copious times when I found my shoulders slumping, my forehead furrowing, and my voice sounding soft and childish. After a few puzzled looks from my husband, whose face was grimacing in concern, I would straighten up and regroup.

We all engage in defense mechanisms, and there are nine that we tend to fall back on. Whether you believe in Freudian's psychosexual theory or not, there's merit to the fact we all have experienced these defense mechanisms. In "The Ego and the Mechanisms of Defense," Sigmund's daughter, Anna Freud, wrote a book listing the defense mechanisms we use:

- DENIAL is failing to accept the truth. An example would be a person with a drinking problem that constantly states, "I'm a social drinker". For victims of trauma or abuse, this can be a helpful defense, but can also have destructive consequences over time.
- REPRESSION is a defense used in forgetting something bad that has happened to you. You might "forget" to go to the dentist. Over time, it can come back to haunt a person, if not confronted.
- DISPLACEMENT involves taking your hurts and pain out on someone or something else, and not addressing the truth. An example could be a physically abused wife kicking the dog, which is a form of displacement.
- PROJECTION is a bit harder to explain. It is when your internal insecurities result in feelings that the people around you are in disapproval. You might blurt out some comment such as, "why are you looking (staring) at me like that?", when there is no ground to support the comment.
- REACTION FORMATION encompasses a defense mechanism whereby one has a deep attraction or

desire but speaks or acts out the exact opposite. An example would be a philanderer who constantly chastises others for the same behavior. Example: The "Church Lady" from Saturday Night Live, who was secretly attracted to pornography, and instead scorned all things of sexual nature.

- INTELLECTUALIZATION involves "outthinking" the situation for your benefit. Suppose your spouse tells you they want a divorce? Rather than break down and cry, you might say, "I can do what I want now, my money will be mine, I will be free to make my own decisions, etc."
- RATIONALIZATION is basically "covering your own butt." When you have demonstrated an undesirable behavior in front of others, you find someone or something else to blame for your mistake. Suppose you have kept a high standard in front of coworkers, and someone drops the coffee pot, and it shatters by your desk. You spout out, "Really?" To defend your reaction, you quickly laugh to hide your initial response. Another example is the abuser that tells the abused, "you knew better, and you had it coming".
- REGRESSION is reverting to another time to avoid the stress in the present. An example would be

retreating under a blanket when things become too stressful. Driving badly or refusing to talk can also be forms of regression.

- SUBLIMATION is a tricky defense mechanism but, in short, involves taking a negative event or series of unwanted events, and choosing behaviors or careers that attempt to correct the unwanted behaviors. Ministers, missionaries, social workers, counselors, doctors, nurses, etc. and many other fields have, at their core, the desire to help others, and perhaps turn their conflicted emotions into something useful and meaningful.

Imagine a room filled with people, all with their own issues, interacting and communicating through defense mechanisms, social norms, mores, and such. We are all impaired to some degree in some area that may well go unaddressed throughout life.

Is there a white elephant that shows up in certain settings of your life? Maybe you are like me, as the white elephant somehow squeezed its way into every crevice of my existence. Perhaps conversations of adultery magnify the white elephant, and you immediately shut down. What about subjects such as liars, cheaters, tax evaders, rape, gossipers? We all have opportunity to clean the

(Susan Krauss Whitbourne Ph.D., The Essential Guide to Defense Mechanisms)

chalkboard that bears the list of sins against us, whether we are the victim or the enforcer.

There is a plethora of approaches to therapy and healing that may or may not bring the desired results in life. One thought that is pervasive in all of us when we think of an elephant is the fact that it is heavy. Imagine for a moment your greatest struggle in life, and that it is contained within the elephant that is immovable by your efforts alone. The pain of constantly having the elephant

> **WE ALL HAVE OPPORTUNITY TO CLEAN THE CHALKBOARD THAT BEARS THE LIST OF SINS AGAINST US, WHETHER WE ARE THE VICTIM OR THE ENFORCER.**

show up might be so unpleasant and yet you dare not reach out and ask for help removing the elephant. You might even become attached to the elephant and feed it with negative and dangerous thoughts of the past. Rather than finding a way to remove the elephant, you continue to allow it to grow and can't seem to see a way of escape.

There is an invitation made by Jesus in Matthew 11:28-30. The Message version states:

"Are you tired? Worn out? Burned out on religion? Get away with me and you'll recover your life. I'll show you how to take a real rest. Walk with me and work with me – watch how I do it. Learn the unforced rhythms of grace. I won't lay anything heavy or ill-fitting on you". The King James Version reads, "Come unto me all ye that labor and are heavy-laden, and I will give you rest. Take my yoke upon you and learn of me; for I am meek and lowly in. heart: and ye shall find rest unto your souls (Mind). For my yoke is easy, and my burden is light."

We are encouraged to leave the elephant (weight, burden) with Jesus. There is no invitation that has ever been or will ever be that holds such a guarantee. Not only will He take the load off, but He alone can also wipe the slate clean in your life, regardless of what has happened in the past whether to you or through you. The vehicle to wipe the slate clean is through FORGIVENESS.

> *"What can wash away my sin,*
> *Nothing but the blood of Jesus*
> *What can make me whole again,*
> *Nothing but the blood of Jesus*
> *O, precious is the flow that makes me white as snow*
> *No other fount I know, nothing but the blood of Jesus*
> (Nothing But The Blood of Jesus / Robert Lowry, 1876)

Come with me on my own journey back home to my father's house . . .

CHAP 14
FATHER, FORGIVE ME

"YOUR FORGIVENESS IS LIKE SWEET,
   SWEET HONEY ON MY LIPS
LIKE THE SOUND OF A SYMPHONY ON MY EARS
IT'S LIKE HOLY WATER ON MY SKIN"

Holy Water (2019), Songwriters: Andrew Bergthold, Franni Cash, Scott Mctyeire Cash, Edward Martin Cash, Edmond Martin Jr Cash

My father's health began to fail in the early 2000's, and he suffered numerous heart surgeries over his last 15 years of life. His strength was failing, but he still seemed to hold a power over me. I would always travel to Alabama when he was scheduled for a surgery. I had this ability to be the perfect daughter and do the right thing. My mother was also suffering with cancer, which originated in 1990. I felt an obligation to repress the past and try to forge out the future.

I recall one multiple by-pass surgery that left my father frail and weak. Mother was resting, and the nurse asked if I would take my father for a walk. He was in a wheelchair, and I was relieved I wouldn't have to look him in the eye. We left the room, past the nurses' station, and turned toward what seemed to be an endless hallway, leading to an arched window from ceiling to floor overlooking the city of Birmingham. There was an eerie silence between us. Inwardly, there was a dialogue in my head. As we approached the window my thoughts were," Look at you now, Daddy. How powerful are you? I am pushing you and you are in my hands. I could just keep pushing and there's nothing you could do." Sadly, he spent the remainder of his life in a mobility scooter to get from one place to another. My trips to Alabama were more frequent than ever, between my father and mother's health. She had faced a mastectomy in 1990, another in 2000, and chemo, radiation, and routine visits to the oncologist for recurring cancer in her bones.

In the fall of 2008, I was asked to speak on the topic of Forgiveness at a weekend seminar. I considered myself an expert on "forgiveness". After all, I had always shared that I had no forgiveness issues toward anyone, so I was the obvious choice on the topic (pun intended). I seemed to be pouring out notes and ideas, scriptures to back it up, and when it came to personal illustrations, all my energy depleted. I had just read Ephesians 4:32 which states, "Be kind and compassionate to one another, forgiving each other, just as in Christ God forgave you. (NIV). I thought little of it, and then early in the next chapter the writer said, "Honor your father and mother, because it is the first commandment that comes with the promise that you will have a long life. (Long, not necessarily in length as much as in quality). Just verses down, the writer is admonishing us to honor our parents.

Never once in my life had I considered myself as dishonoring of my parents, but the truth was that I failed to honor them as parents. It didn't say to honor your worthy, perfect parents. It emphatically said to honor your parents. Why? They are the reason you are here; honor the fact that they were used to bring you into this world so you could accomplish the goals and dreams God has for yourself and your posterity. I realized that all my references to my father in my mind, and even with my husband, were disparaging and maligning. My heart was heavy, and any thought of a possible resolve was rejected as suddenly as it invaded; "Go ask your dad to forgive you for not honoring him as your father." I wanted to curse the thought and say, "Get thee behind me, satan," but it was clear for me that I must pursue this intervention of instruction coming from a higher source than my own. Before nightfall, I was packed and ready to drive 550 miles the next day to release something that had trapped itself deep in my soul for decades. The long drive consisted of doubts, fears, possible negative outcomes, and mostly concerns for what my mother would do. I had boastfully declared for years that I would never hear my father: 1) admit to what he had done or, 2) ask forgiveness for anything!

As I pulled in the driveway unannounced, my father was sitting on the wrap around porch clothed only with his mobility scooter. I called from my cellphone and asked mother to please tell Daddy to put some clothes on. Once inside I asked both parents to sit at the kitchen table. The table was rectangular and positioned within a bay window. My father rolled his mobility scooter to the end closest to the living area. I was on the other end, and Mother was on the side and facing the bay window, in her usual spot. I retrieved a small voice recorder from my pocket and informed them I was recording this event for my posterity and testimony.

My opening words were: "Daddy, this is not about you. This is about me. This is about asking you to forgive me for not honoring you as my father." I looked over to my mother to observe her nose crinkle, her mouth squish together, and her eyes to blink in rhythm to the expression on her face. She placed her hand on mine and was clearly waiting for more information, which I began to disclose. "I have always thought of you as the pervert, the abuser, the person who ruined my life, and I have failed to honor you as my father." Before I could finish the thought, my mother reached over and pulled her hand away. For a moment, I lost eye contact with my father. to check on the welfare of mother. I felt the energy I had draining from me as she withdrew. An implosion of thoughts swirled inside me as I wondered if mother knew, if it was too much to bear, if he was wondering "why now", with both sick and helpless. I momentarily closed my eyes to sort through the tornado within, only to remember a kitchen table much like this one where it all began so many years ago. Only then, his hand was cupped over my mouth, and he had control over me, but now, I had a voice and was using it.

I opened my eyes to the sound of weeping. But it wasn't my mother, as I had suspected. My father's hand was shaking, as was his voice, when he said, "You shouldn't be the one asking me to forgive you. It should be me asking you to forgive me." Mother inserted, "Well do it . . . tell her"! He sounded like a young boy reciting a poem in front of a room of classmates as he spoke very slowly and childish, "Janis, I want you to forgive me." The tornado was silenced as we sat in the aftermath of a life filled with lies, threats, manipulation, suffering, and abuse. Mother reached for Daddy's hand and mine, placed hers on top, and we just sat in the peaceful silence of the moment. I asked if I could say a prayer, and it all ended with "Amen" (amen means so be it).

I hugged them both after our confrontation, and left for Florida, back to my home and family. I left so much baggage in the kitchen that evening. What started in the kitchen had ended in the kitchen. I can't imagine how it must have felt for my father to let go of decades of agony and pain . . . I drove just outside Atlanta and spent the night. I wondered how it would feel to live free from the net that had wrapped itself around me for so long? Something felt different inside and out.

The sun was brightly calling out the next morning. Somewhere between Macon, Georgia, and the Florida state line, I had a deep knowing that the enemy of my soul wanted me dead. I quickly focused on the remarkable series

WHAT STARTED IN THE KITCHEN HAD ENDED IN THE KITCHEN.

of events I had just experienced, but the foreboding kept returning time and again. I was eager to see my husband and share my experience. My husband was in disbelief, and yet filled with gratitude for the miracle that had occurred. Early the next morning, I was showered and dressed at 7:00. Still half asleep, my husband asked, "Where are you going so early?" I exclaimed, "I'm going to Disney world, the Magic Kingdom!" "Where?", he mumbled. "I want to see what it feels like to go somewhere and enjoy life without the heaviness I have carried all my life, and without the huge white elephant that has followed me all these years". I felt like a free child as I passed the sign with Mickey on one side, and Minnie on the other, waving me on. In no time, I was sitting on a bench in Epcot (Experimental Prototype Community of Tomorrow), drinking Starbucks, and experiencing life, rather than observing it.

A greater Kingdom had come from heaven for me. I knew I had allowed the Prince on the white horse to pick me up from the field of daisies, where I had dwelt for so long, and take me on a journey I never thought I could encounter. This adventure replaced the fantasy I had embraced for over 50 years, with a true reality.

Two weeks passed and I was more excited than ever to be decorating for Christmas. I was preparing for the best Christmas I had ever known. Our 12-foot Christmas tree was decorated and only lacked the final topping. I climbed up the 10' ladder and couldn't quite reach the treetop, so I straddled one foot on the fireplace mantle that sits high above the fireplace (in our 25 feet tall living room) and one foot on the top platform of the ladder. My position felt stable until I leaned forward toward the center of the tree. Suddenly, I was tumbling and only had time to say "Go . . . " as an attempt to cry out to God. The last memory was my mouth making contact with the top step of the ladder. I had clinched my mouth and broken 6 teeth in the back, broken my nose, severed my top lip that was hanging by a small piece of skin to one side, broken three ribs, and broken the corner off a granite coffee table with my head. I don't know how long I lay unconscious. My next memory was in an ambulance on the way to the emergency room.

As I emerged into consciousness, I remember saying, "Angels caught me", and at the same time recalled the voice telling me the enemy of my soul wanted me dead. I had not given much thought as to why he wanted me dead. Certainly, the enemy, satan, wants us all dead. What was so significant about me? A startling revelation came that something powerful is released with true forgiveness. It wasn't me, but the process of being the vessel that allowed forgiveness to flow, purging out unforgiveness, bitterness, resentment, hurt, and bringing a healing balm to share with others harboring those unwanted feelings and emotions. A chain reaction had started, and the enemy wanted to extinguish it from continuing.

We often fail to realize we are a conduit for good or evil. I was operating with an ember from heaven that went from me to my father, and from my father to others. If the enemy could put out the fire, he could stop the flow to others in my life. I accepted the challenge and put everything on the table.

My recovery was slow and continued through Christmas of 2008. On February 15, 2009, I received a call on a Sunday afternoon that my father had passed away. I somehow know in my heart he was free, and nothing was holding him back. I flew to Alabama that same night, helped Mother make all the arrangements, and she asked me to sing for the funeral. His favorite gospel song was "Peace in The Valley," recorded by Elvis Presley in 1957. I was only five years old when the song was released. The evening before his service, I found myself studying the lyrics to the song, and couldn't help but notice two lines that stood up on the page like embossing on a state seal. The lyrics are:

> Well, I'm tired and weary But I must go along
> Till the Lord comes to call me away, oh Lord
> Well, the morning is bright, And the Lamb is the Light
> And the night is as fair as the day
>
> Oh, there will be peace in the valley for me, someday
> There will be peace in the valley for me, oh Lord I pray
> There'll be no sadness, no sorrow, no trouble I'll see
> There will be peace in the valley for me, for me
>
> Well, the bear will be gentle
> The wolf will be tame
> And the lion shall lay down with the lamb, oh yes
> And the beast from the wild will be led by a child
> I'll be changed from this creature that I am
>
> Oh, there will be peace in the valley for me some day
> There will be peace in the valley for me, Oh Lord I pray
> There'll be no sadness,
> No sorrow, no trouble I'll see
> There will be peace in the valley for me, for me"

Songwriters: Thomas A. Dorsey. Peace In the Valley lyrics © Warner/Chappell Music, Inc, Tratore

"AND THE BEAST FROM THE WILD WILL BE LED BY A CHILD."

The two lines were: "And the beast from the wild will be led by a child. I'll be changed from this creature that I am." I knew that in God's kingdom, the fragile and innocent child breaks the wild in the beast and changes the creature from what he cannot seem to change for himself.

I was able to mourn the loss in a way that would have been impossible earlier in the previous year. I'm certain the lyrics described the life my father had lived; tired and weary. I prayed he had finally found peace in the valley.

Dr. Athena Stalk, Ph.D., notates "Seven Reasons Forgiveness is Your Nature"

1) It increases your knowledge and understanding of how life works, or doesn't work, to realize more happiness and health, peace and harmony in your relationships. The choice to forgive releases the bonding chemical oxytocin into your bloodstream. Conversely, refusing to forgive releases the stress hormones cortisol. She goes on to say, "It's like taking poison and expecting a hated person to die."

2) It keeps you alive and healthy, preventing you from physical and mental illness and disease. Studies show failing to forgive is associated with disturbances, while forgiving is associated with health benefits.

3) It connects you to your deepest core values, or inner core-emotion drives, to matter and connect to yourself and life in meaningful ways.

4) It fosters your personal and relational growth and transformation. Deep emotion- laden pockets of bitterness, rage and hatred accrue over time.

5) It grows our capacity for compassions for self and others, and life around us. Mother Theresa once said, "If we really want to love, we must learn to forgive."
6) It teaches us to transform our fears into assets. Letting go of bitterness is a gift you give to yourself.
7) It grows your understanding between choices to use fear-based "power" to dominate, limit, force, etc., versus the miracle-making "power" and miracle-making practices to collaborate, inspire, create.

Are you familiar with the Bible story of the Apostle Peter, who approached Jesus with the question, "Lord, how often will my brother sin against me, and I forgive him? As many as seven times?" Jesus said to him, "I do not say to you seven times, but seventy times seven". You might misinterpret this as meaning we are only to forgive 490 times, and that's it! Peter mentioned seven times, hoping to appear generous to Jesus, for the Jewish rabbis taught that one should forgive another three times. They extracted this idea from the book of Amos, whereby God forgave Israel three times, and then sent his wrath upon them. Jesus, in the New Testament, tells Peter essentially, that we continue forgiving others the way God has forgiven us, innumerably.

Once you understand that forgiveness merely flows through you, rather than initiating in you, don't waste another moment of your life, health, or time hesitating to forgive. We are forgiven completely for all our trespasses and sins, and Ephesians 4:32 says we can allow that forgiveness to flow to others in the same way in which we have received it. Another scripture, Matthew 6:16, states, "But if ye forgive not men their trespasses, neither will your Father forgive your trespasses." Wow! This thing starts in Christ, flows to us, flows out to others, and back to Christ. Our choice to forgive releases the power of Christ to forgive us.

You can activate forgiveness, regardless of your position with the person that has offended or abused you. In fact, there is no possibility for health and wholeness outside of forgiveness. I had no courage or strength on my own to make such a giant leap of faith, to ask forgiveness from one who hurt me most in life. I tremble to think I could have lost all opportunity to settle my account should I have waited a few weeks. I had no knowledge that he would die so soon, but I had an urge to set time aside to confront my father and ask forgiveness for myself. I have often wondered, "What if he would have died before I had the opportunity?" I'll never

IT'S DIVINELY FANTASTICAL TO SURRENDER ALL YOUR BROKENNESS IN EXCHANGE FOR ALL OF GOD'S WHOLENESS.

know the answer, but I fully believe I would have taken it to Jesus Christ, and He would have comforted me. Jesus Christ hung on the cross for all the failures you and I have made, and the sins of the whole world. Some of His last words were, "Father, forgive them." You and I are "them", along with all who have sinned against God. He is still willing to make things right if we just say, "Father forgive me of my sins, and come live in my heart". It's divinely fantastical to surrender all your brokenness in exchange for all of God's wholeness.

When I returned home from my father's funeral, I had a dream. I saw a well-dressed and very clean woman standing at the entrance to a dark and ominous mine. As she emerged from the entrance, I could see out, to 10-12 feet piles of coal shavings all around, forming mounds. Standing in front of one of the piles, was a very filthy little girl, with matted hair, sucking her thumb and holding a very dirty and stained doll that was dangling from her other hand. Every part of the girl and doll was stained and dingy. The woman walked as if in slow motion and took the dirty little girl and her doll and kept walking out of the blackness and into the light. She never once turned to look back from where she came. Her head was lifted and confident. The little girl looked up to her as if she were a superwoman. Even in the dream, I was not only an observer, but I knew I was all three. I was the broken child (the stained doll), the broken girl, and the woman. I knew the woman was coming to rescue the broken girl, and the broken child. It was a powerful vision of hope and healing from despair.

With or without a dream, we are all offered an opportunity to emerge from our own darkness and into a new light of living. Ephesians 5:8-13 says, " 8 For you were once darkness, but now you are light in the Lord. Live as children of light 9 (for the fruit of the light consists in all goodness, righteousness and truth) 10 and find out what pleases the Lord. 11 Have nothing to do with the fruitless deeds of darkness, but rather expose them. 12 It is shameful even to mention what the disobedient do in secret. 13 But everything exposed by the light becomes visible—and everything that is illuminated becomes a light."

Take this passage, as did I, and emerge from all darkness that held you down, and held you back from walking in the light. Jesus is the light. Let Him shine and pierce the darkness that has activated you for so long. You may ask, "Where do I even begin?" I knew you would need some guidance, so I have written a special chapter just for you.

CHAP 15
EVER AFTER

" . . . AND THEY LIVED HAPPILY EVER AFTER". These are the final words of most fairytales. Even though we may have experienced mountaintop moments, the story doesn't end on the peak. For new parents, there are bottles to make, diapers to change, crying to soothe and a lifetime of challenges. For newlyweds, there are bills to be paid, work to do, ups and downs, and constant adjustments made in transitioning through life.

For me, I had come full circle with my father and myself. Now, I was on a new path to recover mentally, emotionally, physically, and reach new places spiritually. It was as if I had seen life though cracked eyeglasses, and finally traded them for a brand-new pair. I could see that life was in front of me, but it didn't seem possible it could reach me through the cracked perception by which I had measured everything.

So much of my life had been wasted ruminating over years of events that overtook the positive and good moments from me. Now, I could finally feel proactive and pursue goals and dreams, and destiny. I had enrolled in a community college at age 40, and continued through to my Ph.D. in Psychology from Barry University. Along the way, I became certified as a sexologist, a hypnotist, a master life coach, and a temperament analyst. I was amazed at the rate I could travel through challenges with this heavy load lifted off me. I knew deep inside that obtaining knowledge and education was cathartic and therapeutic for my healing. I became confident that I could share my story with others who had endured similar stories and saw the results each time I stepped forward.

You might be experiencing the freedom

> **PERHAPS YOU ARE WONDERING WHERE TO START ON YOUR ROAD TO RECOVERY. I HAVE HAD YOU IN MIND ALL ALONG AND OFFER SOME SUGGESTIONS THAT MIGHT POINT YOU IN THE RIGHT DIRECTION.**

for yourself as you read along. Perhaps you are wondering where to start on your road to recovery. I have had you in mind all along and offer some suggestions that might point you in the right direction. They are not at all complicated, but effective:

1) Make a list of all your concerns from your past that are hindrances to your future. This is no time for a quick fix. You can begin your list now, or you may first want to consider the ACE quiz below, should you have encountered adverse childhood events that have possibly contributed to interfering with your health and emotional or mental wellness. This assessment is compiled by Drs. Vincent Felitti and Robert Anda, co- founders of the ACE Study. Please read the caveat before deciding to take the quiz. (For the twisted ones like myself, speaking of a caveat only confirms your curiosity to take the quiz).

It has taken this long to arrive at this juncture, now be willing to invest some time to sort through your life and get it right this time. Don't be like two of the Three Little Pigs, who built their houses from straw and wood. When the wolf came, their houses crumbled. But the wise little pig built his house with bricks, and the wolf huffed and puffed, but couldn't blow down his house.

It is much like the parable in Matthew 7:24-27. Jesus tells the crowd, "Therefore whosoever heareth these sayings of mine, and doeth them, I will liken him unto a wise man, which built his house upon a rock: And the rain descended, and the floods came, and the winds blew, and beat upon that house; and it fell not: for it was founded upon a rock. And every one that heareth these sayings of mine, and doeth them not, shall be likened unto a foolish man, which built his house upon the sand: And the rain descended, and the floods came, and the winds blew, and beat upon that house; and it fell: and great was the fall of it." I have given you my heart and soul, and my desire is for you to receive the measure and quality of life I have come to experience. Write down every single event that caused you pain and suffering. Be honest whether you are the offender or the offended. Once you have your list:

2) Take the list and find a quiet place where you feel comfortable and safe. You might even want to make it a ceremony by lighting a candle and playing some soft music in the background. Again, don't rush this

opportunity. Each of these actions will bring you one step closer to healing. Now, pray this prayer: *"Jesus, I don't really know where to start with my life. Thank you for dying on the cross so that I may have abundant life here on earth, and eternal life ever after. I am bringing my concerns to you at your request. You said, "Come unto me and I will give you rest." (Matthew 11:28). I am tired and weary on my own and I am here because I trust and believe you are the only One who can heal my heart and soul."*

3) Take time to grieve over your losses. You can't just pretend they didn't happen and try to move on by ignoring them. If something has affected you, then it is important. No matter how small it may seem in comparison to someone else's struggles, it is yours, and you matter. When there is a physical death, the survivors are encouraged to go for "Grief" counseling. I used the five stages of grief during my healing, and they may be helpful to you. I have added my personal attachments to each area of grief as an example. Please list your own thoughts and feelings.

a. Denial - Well, it didn't hurt me that much. There are so many people worse off than me. It wasn't that bad.

b. Anger - How could they do such a thing to me? They ruined my life. I want them to pay for what they did.

c. Bargaining- Maybe it was my fault, and it wouldn't have happened if I would have been prettier, smarter, or better.

d. Depression - I'll always feel this way and there is nothing that will change how I feel. This is the deck of cards I have been handed, and my life isn't worth living.

e. Acceptance - Come to terms with what you have experienced and allow yourself to grieve the loss. Grieve the broken child, broken girl or boy, broken woman or man, or even the lost relationship. This can take anywhere from a day to a month because it is your personal experiences you are grieving. It can be private or shared with someone you trust. Don't be left too long on your own because we confirm our worse opinions when left to ourselves. We need others to inject options and other ways of looking at situations.

4) Read the list, one by one. Stop after each statement and surrender it over to Jesus. Once you have given it to Jesus, cross it off the list. Don't stop until you have completed the list. It may be one page or many. Perhaps it is just one particular incident, just as my dearest friend experienced. She is my age, and told me that when she was just a young girl, that she stepped up to drink from a water fountain, and a strange man reached up her dress and asked, "what's under there?" She had attended a conference for women, and I shared my personal story. She broke down at the end of my session and told me she had experienced shame all these years since. That night, she was able to check that off her list, as she surrendered that issue at the cross of Jesus.

5) Finish your prayer by saying, *"Now Jesus, these belong to you and not to me. I leave them at the cross and I believe you are healing me from this day forward. Thank you. In Jesus' name."*

6) You can tear up the list, burn it, shred it, but make sure to get rid of it. Those things have no hold on you anymore. It is a supernatural intervention that took your sorrows and burdens and traded them for victory and joy. You don't have to feel it instantly,

although you may. It took all those years for me to get to my place of desperation, and it continues to be a daily choice I make to live with joy and victory. The Bible provides various ways and lengths of times that healings took place.

In Matthew 9:20, there was a lady that had spent every penny on doctors and specialists for a female disorder resulting in constant bleeding. The Bible says that she "thought to herself". This is a profound concept of purposeful positive thinking. She did some self-talk therapy and was convinced if she could touch Jesus, she would be made whole. The story goes on to say he walked down the street with crowds of people following Him, and she shoved her way and grabbed the bottom of his robe and He said, "Daughter, your faith has healed you. Go in peace and be healed from your suffering". For her, it was a snap, and she was healed. The Bible says the blood dried up from that moment on. Another time, in Luke 17:14 two guys were healed as they went back to the priest. Sometimes healing is instantaneous, and in other incidents, it occurs over time. The important thing to know is that you are involved in the process. Jesus told the woman, "Your faith . . . has healed you". Once we know that Jesus is the object of our faith, all things are possible.

God designed our bodies for resilience and to be overcomers through His Son, Jesus. The fallen world seeks to hold us captive from our past and to dim our outlook for the future. The brain can be a powerful source for healing, with its plasticity and ability to renew. The Apostle Paul encourages us to "Be renewed in the spirit of your mind" (Ephesians 4:23). The Greek translation is to be renewed in your mental disposition and attitude. Only Jesus can renew us. Without this renewal, there is little hope for freedom and liberation from past events. When we are left to ourselves, our brain turns on us. Dr. Von der Kolk researched trauma victims and discovered that our body is a scorekeeper. There is a correlation between your memory and the evolving of psychobiology and post-traumatic stress (PTSD). When living with past trauma, the brain sets itself to operate on high-alert mode, depending on the degree of traumatic events involved. This then lends itself to emotional and physical consequences for daily survival, and for casting shadows for future health and wellness issues. It is the difference between seeing the world as malevolent or benevolent.

Failing to adapt to self-regulatory behaviors and living on high-alert has been shown to decrease life-expectancy. Self-regulatory behaviors include:

A) Conscious control of breathing for the purpose of flushing out cortisol, which is a stress hormone. Breathe in slowly through your nose until you feel your lungs expand. Hold the breath for 5 seconds, and then release the air slowly through your slightly opened lips.

B) Dwelling on positives and not negatives. It is as simple as training your brain to quickly speak or think of a positive thought to replace harmful, negative thoughts.

C) Walking, moving, exercising all decrease levels of stress and depression. Research on exercise has proven to be the best way to increase the size of certain parts of the brain that normally decrease with aging and prolongs cognitive functioning.

D) Learn something new by reading, researching, studying the Bible. Learning promotes neuronal branching and new neurons are generated (neurogenesis). New neurons are also reinforced (neuroplasticity) when we are learning. The brain continues to change throughout one's lifespan, unlike information we were given just decades ago.

Below is the ACE (Adverse Child Experiences) Quiz. It is designed to provide a number that correlates with a person's risk for chronic disease, as well as life expectancy. Drs. Feletti and Anda were working with a population of obese patients and discovered a high rate of dropout despite effective weight loss. From their survey, they discovered many dropouts consisted of those who had suffered sexual abuse as a child. They felt weight gain was a coping mechanism for depression, anxiety, and fear. *As a caveat, the ACE focuses on traumatic and negative events from childhood, and none of the positive mechanisms used for resilience and coping. There is much discussion about incorporating more positives to accompany this test.

ACE QUIZ

While you were growing up, during your first 18 years of life:

1) Did a parent or other adult in the household often . . .

    Swear at you, insult you, put you down, or humiliate you?

    or

    Act in a way that made you afraid that you might be physically hurt?

    o Yes   o No   If yes, enter 1____

2) Did a parent or other adult in the household often . . .

    Push, grab, slap, or throw something at you?

    or

    Ever hit you so hard that you had marks or were injured?

    o Yes   o No   If yes, enter 1____

3) Did an adult or person at least 5 years older than you ever . . .

    Touch or fondle you or have you touch their body in a sexual way?

    or

    Try to or have oral, anal, or vaginal sex with you?

    o Yes   o No   If yes, enter 1____

4) Did you often feel that . . .

No one in your family loved you or thought you were important or special?

or

Your family didn't look out for each other, feel close to each other, or support each other?

    o Yes   o No   If yes, enter 1____

5) Did you often feel that . . .

You didn't have enough to eat, had to wear dirty clothes, and had no one to protect you?

or

Your parents were too drunk or high to take care of you or take you to the doctor if you needed it?

    o Yes   o No   If yes, enter 1____

6) Were your parents ever separated or divorced?

    o Yes   o No   If yes, enter 1____

7) Was your mother or stepmother:

Often pushed, grabbed, slapped, or had something thrown at her?

or

Sometimes or often kicked, bitten, hit with a fist, or hit with something hard?

or

Ever repeatedly hit over at least a few minutes or threatened with a gun or knife?

    o Yes   o No   If yes, enter 1____

8) Did you live with anyone who was a problem drinker or alcoholic or who used street drugs?

    o Yes   o No   If yes, enter 1____

9) Was a household member depressed or mentally ill or did a household member attempt suicide?

    o Yes   o No   If yes, enter 1____

10) Did a household member go to prison?

    o Yes   o No   If yes, enter 1____

Now add up your "Yes" answers: _____

Now that you have your ACE score, you may be interested in knowing: The higher your ACE score, the higher your risk for sickness, disease, and life expectancy. This test originated with CDC (Center for Disease Control) and included a population of people diagnosed with obesity. The instructors noticed a high rate of dropouts in the program, despite the success in weight lose that was occurring within the group. It was not specifically designed for mental health counselors. A correlation between health and adverse childhood experiences (ACE) became the focus of a study in the 1990's, which is used with mental health counselors, therapists, health care providers, and social workers. There are many other groups utilizing the ACEs approach with Law Enforcement, prison inmates, etc. In 1995-97, a study including upwards of 17,000 people participated in the ACE quiz. (Adverse Childhood Experiences). People with a score of six or more on the ACES's survey died 20 years earlier than those with no score.

References

The 5 Stages of Grief & Loss
By Julie Axelrod psychcentral.com Adverse Childhood Experiences and the Risk of Premature Mortality
November 2009Volume 37, Issue 5, Pages 389–396
Van der Kolk B. The body keeps the score. New York: Viking; 2014. [PubMed]
Mental Retirement." Rohwedder, S. & Willis, R. 2010. Journal of Economic Perspectives 24(1):119-38. NIHMS. doi: 10.1257/jep. 24.1.119.

Janis, age 3.

Janis and Michael with their Maw-Maw.

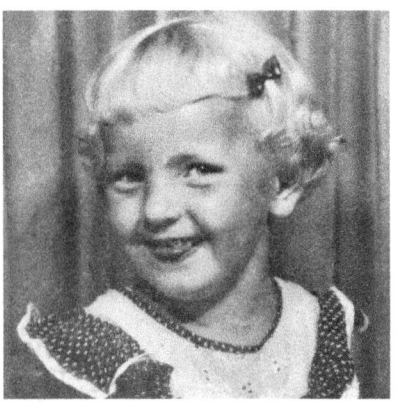
Age 4

Brother looking out with sister.

Janis, Age 5.

School days.

In front of the house in the mining camp. Age 8.

THANKS TO RESCUER FROM BURNING SLATE
... Janise Kay Flippo (right) has flowers for Raymond Burrell

Wades through hot slate—
Heroic student saves tot from fiery death

BY CHARLES GRAINGER
News staff writer

A barefoot boy, fresh from a dip in "the swimmin' hole," had his peaceful rest cut short by a scream.

That scream made of him: A hero.

And a patient at a hospital

Fifteen-year-old Raymond Burrell, of Sayre, Saturday was credited with possibly saving the life of a neighboring child.

Janise Kay Flippo, 6, had been picking "poke salad" near the slate-dump at Sayre when she wandered into the danger area where slate fires burned beneath the topsoil.

Her bare feet began burning. She screamed for help.

RAYMOND, basking in the sun in his backyard near the dump, spotted the youngster. No time now to put on shoes left off after his swimming trip.

He dashed to the foot of the 100-foot slope. Halfway up, the child screamed, "Help, somebody! Come help me!"

The burning sulphuric slate, covered only by a thin coating of topsoil—with craterlike crevices
Turn to Page 2 Column 4

Part of the Birmingham News article about Janis' rescue from the fiery slate dump.

Clacker from the Sayre Coal Mines Commissary.

Sayre Coal Mines workers.

Janis' mother drove off of a bridge like this.

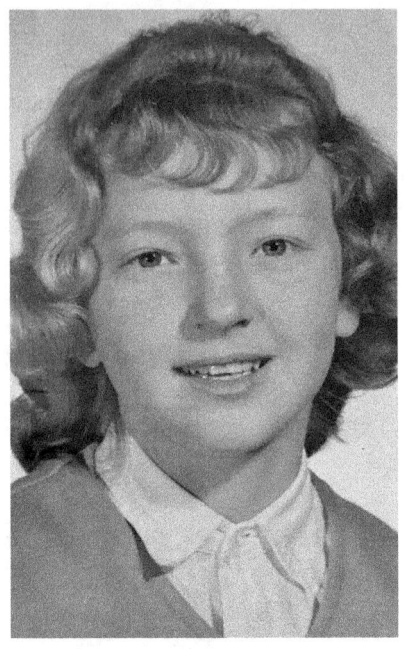

Age 12

Age 13

*Age 15, with Michael,
Hammond, Indiana*

When Michael graduated. 1968

Hammond, Indiana

In front of the Hammond, Indiana house

Janis with Michael at a convention.

The wedding gown that drug through the mud.

Newlyweds

"The SOULSEARCHERS" (our Music Evangelistic Team) traveled in Revival Crusades across the country.

Newlyweds in National Evangelism.

Early pastoral days in Florida.

Early pastoral days in Florida.

Dr. Janis Smith

My grandfather's testimony of healing.

Proof That God Heals

Brother George Flippo of Praco, Alabama, writes his own story of God's power to heal him instantly. His story follows:

"On February 3, 1938, I was seriously injured in a mine accident, being dragged through a place which seemed impossible for a person of my size to go through. I was knocked unconscious for about five minutes. When I regained consciousness I was calling on the Lord, reminding the Lord of how I had been a member of the Church of God and had stood to His Word and trusted the healing power of the Lord for more than five years. My fellow workmen all gathered around and tried to do something for me. Some tried to administer shots and ammonia but I resisted all medicine and medical aid, fully trusting the Lord who can heal when none can hinder. Praise the Lord. As I prayed and cried out to God, those around me who were for the most part hardened sinners, bowed in reverence and tears streaked their faces that were black already from toil.

They put me on a stretcher and carried me outside to the Doctor's office where I went through another round of resisting medical aid. The doctor said that if I lived to reach the hospital I would not live over five days. He tried to give me a shot in the arm to lessen the misery and suffering, but I refused, telling him that Jesus suffered for me and that I was willing to suffer for Him if it were His will.

The Mine Superintendent tried to get me to yield to medical aid by flattery and sweet talk, but I told him that I stood four square for divine healing just like God's Bible taught. He said afterward that he had no more to say against divine healing and before this he was against the Church of God and holiness.

When they got me to the hospital they made X-ray pictures and examined me thoroughly and found my left leg to be broken two inches below the hip joint, the pelvis broken and a torn place in the neck of the bladder.

The attendants at the hospital tried to get me to take medicine and shots but I resisted it again. Each time I resisted medical aid the Lord would touch my body and remove the pain. After the nurses and doctors saw that I intended to stand firm for divine healing they were nice about it and didn't try to force medicine on me any more.

I called for the elders of the church and requested prayer and the saints continued holding on to the Lord until we got victory. On Monday night, February 7th, just four days later, the Lord healed my body, made me completely whole. I told the other patients that I was healed and could walk and they laughed and scorned, but I knew that the dear Lord had done just what He promised. Praise His name.

I was clad only in a night shirt and couldn't get out of bed before the lady nurses, but when the nurses went off duty and were replaced by men nurses, I got up and walked to prove to all present that I was healed. They all called me crazy and told me that I'd kill myself. I asked the doctor about going home and he said that I'd be in the hospital for six or seven more weeks, but praise the Lord, I was there only eleven days in all. I came home February 14th, and have been in the work of the Lord ever since."

Approved by Committee on Doctrine

Order this tract by No. 6008.

White Wing Publishing House & Press
P.O. Box 1039, Cleveland, Tenn.

connect with
DR. JANIS

For further information on the ministry of Dr. Janis Smith, including music, books, and other resources, scan the QR code.

- drjanis
- drjanissmith
- angelstrail.com

www.ingramcontent.com/pod-product-compliance
Lightning Source LLC
LaVergne TN
LVHW051827080426
835512LV00018B/2760